Introduction to insurance

By Gordon C A Dickson M.Litt., Ph.D., FCII.

1984

STUDY COURSE 010

THE CII TUITION SERVICE

This is a coursebook of the CII Tuition Service
of 31 Hillcrest Road, London, E18 2JP
a division of the Education & Training Trust
of the Chartered Insurance Institute
of 20 Aldermanbury, London, EC2V 7HY

ISBN 0–907323–66–9

THE AUTHOR

Dr Dickson is senior lecturer in risk management at Glasgow College of Technology. Before entering the world of education he had a number of years' experience in the insurance industry. He has spent some time working and carrying out research in the United States of America. In addition to this text he has written and contributed to a number of books on insurance and risk management and has contributed regularly to the insurance press. He is a Fellow of the Chartered Insurance Institute and a graduate of the University of Glasgow.

ADDITIONAL READING

A number of texts are mentioned at various points throughout this book, to which the interested reader can refer. In addition to this, student readers should keep up-to-date by reading insurance magazines such as Post Magazine and Insurance Monitor.

Produced for the CII by Book Production Consultants,
47 Norfolk Street, Cambridge
and printed in England by The Burlington Press (Cambridge) Limited,
Foxton, Cambridge

Contents

It is intended that books in this series will be reissued in new editions as necessary. In order to keep this process as economical as possible the system has been adopted of numbering the pages in each chapter in a separate sequence. Thus each page bears a composite number, in which the number before the stroke indicates the chapter, and the number after the stroke indicates the page within that chapter.

1. The nature of risk

1A.The concept of risk

One frequently hears on television or radio of some major fire or explosion or earthquake in some foreign country, a multiple collision on one of our motorways or a workman falling to his death at a nearby building site. Hardly a day passes without stories like these being reported.

Newspapers, too, carry similar items. It is common to see headlines dealing with fires, robberies, aeroplane crashes, oil spillages and many other similar incidents.

Such events are so common that they rarely occupy the front pages of our newspapers, but occasionally there is some occurrence that does make front page news possibly due to the cost involved or the loss of life. Whether we are thinking of the extremely large incident or the thousands of others reported annually in our press we have become used to hearing about them.

For all of us the risk that we might be involved with one of these events is always present. We may be in a car accident, our house may be robbed or damaged by fire, or we might suffer some illness which prevents us from working. Businesses are similarly confronted with risks. Factories may be destroyed by fire, valuable stock could be stolen, computer records damaged or injury caused to innocent people.

Behind all the events we have mentioned lies a great deal of anxiety and grief, as can be imagined, for those closely involved. What many people do not realise is that a vast, sophisticated mechanism also lies behind each risk which, if properly used, can greatly alleviate the financial hardship which may have been caused.

That mechanism is insurance and this text book is an introduction to what you will come to appreciate as the extremely important, challenging and exciting role insurance plays in our modern society.

Risk is at the very centre of insurance and before moving on to examine the latter in more detail it is essential that we understand fully the concept of risk.

1A1.Definitions of risk

In addition to being at the centre of insurance, risk is also at the centre of life itself and as a result many people from different walks of life are concerned with it. Economists, doctors, psychologists, business men, philosophers, engineers, scientists and many others all have an interest in the concept of risk.

The widespread nature of the interest in risk is matched only by the many definitions of risk which have been offered. Here are just a few which have been put forward by scholars over the years:

— Risk is the objective doubt concerning the outcome in a given situation.
— Risk is the uncertainty as to the occurrence of an economic loss.
— Risk is unpredictability, the tendency that actual results may differ from predicted results.
— Risk is the possibility of an unfortunate occurrence.
— Risk is the chance of loss.
— Risk is a combination of hazards.

Each one of these definitions has appeared in risk and insurance textbooks and each is supported by its respective author and is not so well received by the others. Clearly there can be no one authoritative definition of risk in the sense that it will find universal acceptance. It is necessary, however, for us to generate a working definition which will serve for the purposes of this book and act as a foundation for the future study of insurance.

We will look upon risk as the uncertainty of loss. This definition has the advantage of being brief but in addition has some merit over the others listed above. It avoids introducing too many undefined and possibly ambiguous words such as 'doubt', 'objective', 'unpredictability', 'possibility' and 'hazard'. Our definition is restricted to the two ideas of uncertainty and loss. It avoids situations where no likelihood of loss exists and also those situations which will definitely happen.

PARENTS WERE SWEPT AWAY

By NIGEL BENSON

Car crash death

A TEENAGE boy died and another was injured today after a stolen car crashed in West Belfast. Police said the dead youth had been thrown out of the car when it hit a lamp standard. The car had been stolen.

The victim as yet unidentified was the second to be killed in incidents involving stolen cars in over the past four days.

On Friday Patrick McNally (20) by an Ulster Defence Regiment chase, and on Saturday a youth injuries after the stolen car a security bollard.

Arson causes new tragedy £100m loss

LAST year in Britain, the total cost of fire damage was £355.3m. This figure, estimated by the British Insurance Association, shows a marked increase on the 1978 figure of £309.3m and indicates an average cost of nigh on £1m a day.

...d not succeed and then I got ... of the boat."

had a paddle, so ...turned hull they ...na.

...e drifting to ... weather, ... light

COPTER CRASH PROBE

INVESTIGATORS ...ay began a ...obe into a helicop-crash which ...ed four ... the

Lost At Sea

...nthony Renouf previews a new ...ulent going

have its $56m cargo ripped off ...clandestine South

Fox fur stolen

ABOUT 3 p.m. on Monday of this week, a thief broke into a car parked in West Nile Street at West Regent Street, Glasgow, and stole a lady's blue fox fur jacket.

The jacket, which is a size 10, had a mandarin ... and a grey silk lining. It is valued at £550 and ... Sergeant Pile of Stewart Street CID is in ... the investigation. Anyone who can assist ...ntact him at 041 332 1113.

POLICE FLASHES

example, for Ms that when it gets country the would like f instan ...rin

Bearsden house is raided

...to a ...en ...arch Wed-
...g evening.
...p.m. the
...removed two Sony
recorders model num-
...s TC377 and TC280

...nt's gold wedding ring ...h the maker's initials ...stamped inside the

...y information about ...break-in or any of the ...es to Det.-Ser ...nt at Bear ...one

COUPLE ESCAPE BLAZE IN FLAT

A WOMAN had a narrow escape early today when her bed caught fire.

But Mrs Mary Duffy (62) was able to raise the alarm in time as flames licked around the bedroom of her top-floor flat in Risk Street, Dumbarton.

Husband Dickie Duffy ...7) managed to push his ...fe out of the door to ...ety as smoke belched ...und them.

... Duffy — who played ...all for Falkirk, Alloa, ... Motherwell in his ... — said later...

'The bed's on fire.'
"I managed to calm her and push her out of the door as flames leapt out the bedroom."
Firem...

...sive smoke dam... house and...

out in her first-floor flat at 21 Dougrie Place.
She saw smoke coming from an airing cupboard. Her grandson, Michael McGowan (17), was asleep in another bedroom as smoke engulfed the rooms. Michael was detained ... Glasgow's Vict... mary t...

Figure 1/1 shows a number of newspaper clippings and from these we can see how our definition can apply. The uncertainty of loss in these clippings ranges over personal injury, fire damage, helicopter crashes, theft of belongings etc. Each one describes a loss and in each case this loss was not certain to occur; in other words there was some uncertainty of loss.

1A2. Uncertainty and certainty

This sense of uncertainty surrounds everything we do in life. We do not know if we will pass an exam, if we will succeed in the job interview, if we will gain promotion and so on. In a business sense uncertainty is no less important.

Almost everything the business man does he does in an uncertain environment. If he invests in new machinery, will the output be what is expected, will the employees be prepared to work with it, what is the delivery of parts situation? If he launches a new product will it sell as expected? Will a new bonus scheme for employees avoid a threatened strike? If he builds a new factory will it burn down? Will thieves steal his finished products from the warehouse?

In a few cases he knows, with certainty, what the future holds. He knows that if he reduces the number of machines used his fuel bill will come down. If he employs four new people he knows that his payroll will increase. Most of his activities, however, still involve him in venturing forward in this atmosphere of uncertainty.

It is valuable that we recognize, at this early stage, the omnipresent nature of uncertainty and that, faced with uncertainty, life, both personal and business, continues day by day.

1B. Forms of risk

The emphasis on the word 'loss' in our definition of risk highlights the fact that we are concerned with those risks which hold out the prospect of some loss that is capable of financial measurement. With this in mind we can discuss two separate dichotomies of risk; and then introduce the idea of hazard.

1B1. Pure and speculative

We have looked at the pervasive nature of risk both in private and business contexts but even when we have limited our study of risk to those situations which involve a potential loss there is one further distinction that must be made.

To have a situation that involves a loss we could imagine two combinations of situations.

The first form of situation holding out the prospect of a loss could be where either a loss or a break-even position may materialize. Driving a motor car represents an example of this. Every time you take your car on the road you run a risk; there is the uncertainty of loss. You may damage your car or other property or incur a liability in view of injury sustained by someone. Should you get home free of incident then we could say you have broken even.

The second situation is where you may experience a loss, break-even or a profit. A good example of this kind of risk is evidenced by the stock market and those who buy shares. You may purchase shares at 25p. each and a year later they may only be worth 20p. On the other hand they may not have changed value and could still stand at 25p. What you hope, of course, is that they have risen in price so that when you want to sell them you will profit by the sale.

These two types of event are termed, respectively, pure and speculative risks. A pure risk holds out the prospect of a loss or no loss while a speculative risk holds out the prospect of a gain as well as loss or break-even.

In the business world speculative risks are very common. Exporting to a new market, launching a new product and fixing retail prices are all forms of speculative risk as they hold out the prospect of loss, break-even or profit. Pure risks are equally common. The factory may burn down, profit may be lost following a fire, money may be stolen. These situations hold out the prospect of loss but at the same time they may not occur and the result will be the *status quo*. It is important to realize that the firm does not gain solely through the fact that the factory did not burn, that profit was not lost following a fire or that money was not stolen; it simply maintains the *status quo* or, as we have said earlier, has broken even.

1B2. Fundamental and particular

A further method of classifying risks is to divide them into fundamental and particular risks. A fundamental risk is one that is impersonal both in origin and consequence. The losses that flow from fundamental risks are not normally caused by one individual and their impact generally falls on a wide range of people.

Rather than talk of fundamental risks it may be helpful to refer to risks of a fundamental nature. They are termed fundamental as they arise out of the nature of the society we live in or from some physical occurrence beyond the control of man. Examples of such risks are war, inflation, changing customs, typhoons and tidal waves, the first three arising out of the kind of society we have and the last two being attributable to some physical occurrence.

A particular risk, or a risk of a particular nature, has its origin in individual events and its impact is felt locally. Theft of property, accidental damage to personal effects and explosion of a boiler are particular risks.

1B2A. Changes in classification

Attitudes change over time and there are examples of risks moving from one classification to another. The most common alteration in classification has been from particular to fundamental and this gives some hint as to why we bother classifying risks at all. Before looking at this question let us take two examples of risks changing classification.

Unemployment, at one time, was looked upon as the fault of the individual concerned. It may have arisen out of his laziness, lack of training or a host of reasons but unemployment was very much a particular risk. Over many years the view of society has changed and today most people would agree that unemployment arises out of some malfunctioning of the economic system. In this way the risk has changed to be one of a fundamental nature, not attributable to any individual, and widespread in its consequences.

Motor accidents represent another area of risk where changes are taking place. The popular view for a long time has been that a motor accident is brought about by the fault of one person and the legal systems in most countries acknowledge this by having a system of compensation that relies on the person who has suffered injury, or who has had property damaged, proving that the driver was to blame. Gradually, however, this view is altering and some people are beginning to wonder if it would not be more accurate to think of the motor accident as having arisen due to a combination of events, not all of which are within the control of the driver. Evidence of this change is found in those countries where state compensation exists, without proof of fault.

These two examples do, as indicated earlier, provide some clue as to why it is necessary to have the particular and fundamental dichotomy. When a risk is looked upon as being of a fundamental nature, the Government has normally taken notice of the views of society and stepped in with some scheme to provide compensation for victims, for example, by means of unemployment benefit.

1B3. Physical hazard

Physical hazard relates to the physical or tangible aspects of the risk which are likely to influence the occurrence and/or severity of loss.

Aspects which are likely to increase the likelihood of loss or its severity compared with an average risk are termed poor or unfavourable physical hazards. Similarly, aspects which are likely to reduce the incidence of loss or the potential severity can be regarded as good physical features. Perhaps the easiest way in which to understand these features is to give examples from several types of risk.

1B3A. Fire

Methods of construction which are liable to add fuel to a fire rather than contain it would be bad features e.g., timber walls or thatched roofs. The storage of dangerous chemicals, oils, packaging materials, or the use of naked lights such as blow-torches or even smoking are other examples.

Good physical features would include brick or concrete fire-stop walls and metal fire doors, automatic sprinkler and alarm systems, and the segregation of dangerous processes and goods from the less dangerous areas of a factory. However, the accidental leakage of water from a sprinkler installation may do more damage to some commodities e.g., paper products such as books, than would a fire.

1B3B. Theft

A building having lightweight construction walls or roof such as timber, asbestos, or corrugated iron, or normal window catches and rim latches on doors would present several poor features offering little resistance to a potential intruder. Additionally if the contents of a building are attractive to thieves e.g., jewellery, wines and spirits, tobaccos, non-ferrous metals, the risk would be regarded as being heavy in physical hazard.

Strong building construction, security locks and bolts and intruder alarm systems can greatly improve what would otherwise be a poor physical risk.

1B3C. Motor accidents

The use of a vehicle in areas of high traffic density such as London, Glasgow and similar large cities increases the likelihood of an accident. The use of a vehicle for certain trades is likely to mean it being on the road for most of the day with similar consequences e.g., a taxi or a representative's car. Cars which are costly to repair such as a Rolls Royce or a Mercedes could be regarded as presenting extra hazard. Drivers under the age of 25 and sports cars are often regarded as poor physical risks, but it may be more correct to regard them as high moral hazards (see later).

1B3D.Liability The use of chemicals, oils, and the creation of dusts and vapours in industrial processes represent adverse physical hazards to employees but these can be reduced substantially by protective clothing, goggles and masks, and by the use of extraction fans and ducting. Potential liability to the public is increased where work is done in customers' premises, particularly if heat is used e.g. cutting and welding with the use of gas burners.

1B3E.Marine risks The use of poorly equipped or maintained vessels, stowage of cargo on deck and bad packing are examples of poor physical hazard.

1B3F.Personal health A history of recurring illness, hazardous occupations such as coal mining or deep sea diving are examples in these fields, as is a person excessively overweight.

1B4.Moral hazard Moral hazard is concerned with the attitudes and conduct of people. In insurance, this will be primarily the conduct of the person insured, but the conduct of his employees and society at large have an ever-increasing influence in assessing moral hazard. Moral hazard is just as important as physical hazard, if not more so, in influencing the cost of loss.

1B4A.The insured (the person or firm insuring) The most serious example of bad moral hazard on the part of the insured is the person who submits false or exaggerated claims. Another example is where information necessary for the proper assessing of the risk is withheld or misrepresented either deliberately or innocently.

By far the most common example of poor moral hazard is that of carelessness: the insured who fails to take reasonable care to prevent loss or damage to his property, or for the safety and wellbeing of his employees and others. This often arises through other pressures of business and domestic life appearing to be more important, or the insured may be totally ignorant that his or her conduct is increasing the likelihood of loss. The only really satisfactory way in which to improve moral hazard is to educate the insured in the potential dangers and how to reduce them.

It is sometimes difficult to draw a dividing line between physical and moral hazard. A sports car was quoted above as an example of a poor physical risk, but such a car by itself cannot cause more accidents than a family saloon and some of them represent less value than a saloon. It is the manner in which it is driven which is the hazard as most purchasers of sports cars wish to use their speed, sometimes with disastrous results. Very often when a physical hazard exists, e.g., unsafe working conditions, it is only the result of poor moral hazard at an earlier stage. For example, in planning the factory or in supervising its operations, these unsafe conditions may have been created when safer procedures could easily have been incorporated.

A final example of poor moral hazard in the insured is the arrogant and 'awkward' individual. This is often evident at the proposal stage and it is likely that he will be even harder to deal with at the time of a claim. In practice it is unlikely that the insurer or broker can improve the risk and declinature may be the best course of action for all concerned.

1B4B.Employees If management/employee relationships are poor or if it is the custom in the trade that wage levels are very low, there is likely to be little incentive on the part of the employee to be careful in his or her work. In extreme cases there may be sabotage, vandalism, or wilful fire raising.

1B4C.Society We must always be conscious of the attitudes of society at large as these can influence the level of risk and the incidence of claims. In recent years there has been increasing incidence of vandalism and wilful fire raising. In certain parts of the country fires caused deliberately have been the largest single cost of any identified source of fire damage. Insureds are also becoming more claims-conscious, and the result of these trends is, in the case of house insurance at least, that rates have been increased by up to 100% in the last few years in order to keep those accounts in profit.

1C.The dimensions of risk What we have said so far is fairly theoretical. Let us try now to relate our ideas of risk to the real world. One thing we could attempt to do is to evaluate the size of any problem which the existence of risk may cause. We cannot look at every single form of risk which exists but if we take a few examples we may be able to form some view as to how important risk is.

Road Accidents. In 1982 there were 334,296 road casualties of which 5,934 were fatally injured, 79,739 seriously injured and 248,623 were slightly injured. The Road Research Laboratory has worked out that the cost to the country of *each* fatal road accident, expressed in 1983 pounds, is approximately:

	£
Lost output	74900
Police and administration	300
Medical and ambulance	600
Property damage	1640
	77440
Pain and suffering	51760
	129200

This paints a very clear picture of the importance of this one form of risk.

Fire Damage. Fire is a major risk with which industry and private individuals must come to terms. In 1983 the total cost of damage to property caused by fire was £565.6m. This figure includes all material damage loss whether it was covered by an insurance policy or not. It does not take into account the loss to the economy as a whole, brought about by the disruption of a fire, such things as loss of production, lost markets etc. If we add on these additional, consequential, losses the figure would be many times higher than £565.6m.

Figure 1/2 shows how the fire waste figure has moved over the past ten years.

Figure 1/2 Fire waste figures

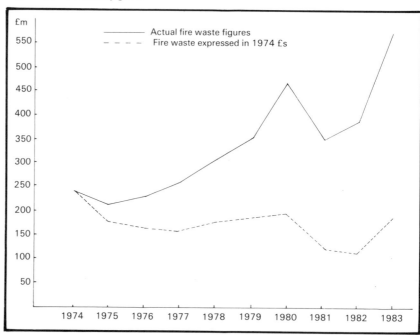

Source: BIA Facts and Figures

The top line shows the actual fire waste figures over the last ten years. This line, of course, also includes the effect of inflation. In periods of relatively high inflation then it costs progressively more to pay for the same amount of fire damage. One simple way to illustrate this is to think of a £30,000 house which was totally destroyed by fire in January 1983. If it was possible to rebuild that house immediately then the cost would be £30,000. If exactly the same house had been destroyed one year later in January 1984 and rebuilt immediately then the cost would be more, due only to the reduction in the value of money. If we assume that inflation had been 5% over the period then the cost of rebuilding would be £31,500 (£30,000 + 5%). You can see here that the increase in the cost of that particular piece of fire damage is due to inflation and not in fact to more extensive fire damage.

Translate this simple example to all fire damage in the country. Any increase in fire damage will be due partly to inflation and possibly also to an increase in fire damage itself. This latter form of increase we can refer to as a *real* increase.

The broken line on our graph has expressed fire damage in 1974 £'s and hence has removed the influence of any change in the value of money. Movements in the line must be due to *real* increases or decreases in fire damage. Looking at this broken line we can see that fire damage did increase in *real* terms over the period 1977 to 1980, then decreased before rising again in 1983.

These peaks in 1980 and 1983 can be explained by delving a little bit more deeply into the fire waste figures. In 1980 there were two substantial fires: a fire at British Aerospace which cost £72.5m and also the Alexandra Palace fire which cost £30m. In today's terms these fires would have cost a total of approximately £140m. In 1983 a single fire costing £165m occurred at an Army Ordnance Depot in England and if it had not been for that, the fire waste figures may have continued to decrease in *real* terms.

We have spent rather a long time on fire damage but, as you can see, it is an extremely important aspect of risk. Any risk, which costs almost £18 per second or £10 for every man, woman and child in the country, is worth spending a little time on.

Industrial Accidents. In 1981 we lost 384.8 million days work in industry from all causes. Of this total figure, 36m or 9% were due to industrial accidents. This figure is three times larger than the number of days lost through strikes in the same year and represents a considerable drain on industry.

When men or women are involved in industrial accidents there is inevitably a stoppage of work with consequent loss of production, possible damage or loss to products or machines, the need to replace injured persons etc.

Not all industrial accidents result in a payment to injured employees but for those where such a payment was involved, insurance companies paid approximately £191.6m in 1981.

Crime. Another form of risk is that where you suffer loss due to the criminal acts of some other person. In 1982, for example, there were 800,267 thefts of or from motor vehicles, 407,088 burglaries in dwellings and 983,620 other forms of thefts and robberies.

Excluding motor vehicle thefts, which we know to be considerable, insurance companies paid £235.3m in 1982 for crime losses.

What these few examples are intended to illustrate is the magnitude of the problems posed by risk, and, as we said in 1A, behind these figures lies a great deal of personal suffering and tragedy which anyone who has been the victim of risk will confirm.

1D. Analysing risk

The fact that uncertainty of loss abounds has resulted in a great deal of effort being devoted to its measurement over many years. In measuring risk we try to place some value on our belief as to the likelihood that some event will or will not occur.

1D1. Frequency and severity

In conversation people may refer to an event as risky or not too risky and in this way give some indication of their own degree of belief. What, however, is meant by the word risky?

Take as an example the risk of fire damage in a storeroom at a factory. A person may refer to the prospect of fire damage as being very risky, but does he mean there is a very strong likelihood of a fire, or that it is unlikely there will be a fire but if it happens it will result in a very high financial loss?

In other words, when we talk of risk we must be clear in our minds that it incorporates both the frequency with which an event may take place and the severity of each incident which does occur.

The operation of a chemical plant is very risky, not because these installations have frequent losses but because when a loss does take place it involves a very high financial amount. The explosion at the Flixborough plant in 1974 is a good example of this point. The opposite could be the case where a large department store considers the breakage of glass windows to be very risky. They are not referring to the cost of each broken window but to the frequency with which windows are broken and the fact that in aggregate the cost of broken glass is high.

This concept of frequency and severity is one which is well known in the risk and insurance world. The relationship between frequency and severity, in insurance, is usually that there is a high frequency of low severity incidents and a low frequency of high severity incidents. For example, in the case of household fires there are very many small incidents of fire damage but very few cases where houses are destroyed completely.

This is illustrated in figure 1/3 (a) where we see that high frequency is associated with low severity.

In figure 1/3 (b) we show the opposite case of high frequency being associated with high severity. One risk which may be explained by this shape would be, for example, aviation insurance, since aviation accidents are more likely to cause total losses than small incidents.

This relationship between frequency and severity also applies to industrial accidents.

There is a well known diagram referred to as the 'Heinrich Triangle'. This is illustrated in figure 1/4.

The 'Heinrich Triangle' shows that for every one major injury there are 30 minor injuries and 300 non-injury accidents. This triangle was the result of studying several thousand incidents and helps to reinforce what we have already said about frequency and severity. The most frequent industrial accident is the accident involving no injury, possibly a 'near miss' or some property damage. The most infrequent incident is the one involving a major injury.

Figure 1/3 Frequency and severity

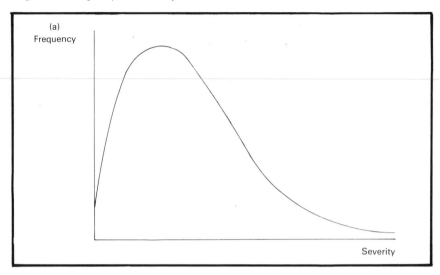

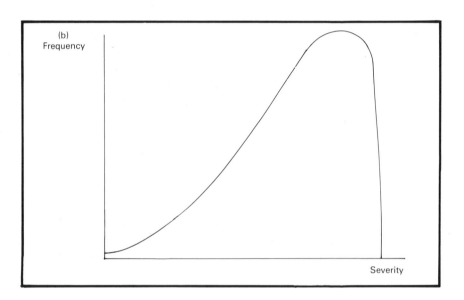

Figure 1/4 Heinrich triangle

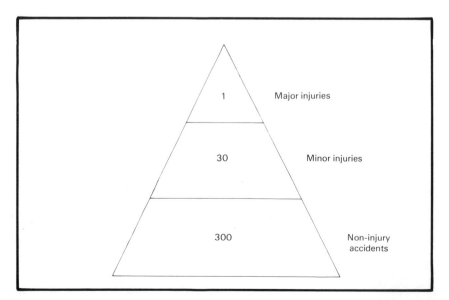

1D2. Statistical risk analysis

In measuring the frequency and severity of risk we are brought into close contact with the world of statistics. Insurance is particularly fortunate as it generates large volumes of figures which makes our statistical calculations much easier than it would be if we were working with no experience of the past.

Statistics is there to assist our analysis of risk and is a tool which is used to great effect. The whole range of statistics can be divided roughly into two sections, descriptive and inferential.

1D2A. Descriptive statistics

This branch of statistics deals with the systematic collection of information, its presentation and description.

Let us say you are an insurance company concerned by the high level of motor accident claims experienced over recent years. You decide to analyse this risk and start by collecting information about the cost of motor accidents. This collection of data has to be planned carefully and executed efficiently. One way of collecting information on the cost of motor accidents would be to ask the computer, on which you probably store such information, to provide a breakdown of the cost of claims. You may wish this cost broken down into those accidents involving private cars, commercial vehicles and buses. Alternatively, you may wish to compare different areas of the country. Assuming that the relevant information is stored in the first place then it should be possible to extract what you want.

Having thought about the data you wish to collect, it is then necessary to represent what you have found in a manner which will illustrate clearly the main features. A whole range of techniques can be employed, some of which are used at various stages throughout this book. A simple graph may be used to illustrate how claims figures have moved. We have already seen this in figure 1/2 when we looked at fire waste figures. In addition to the graph we could represent our data with any one of the following techniques shown in figure 1/5.

Figure 1/5 Representation of data

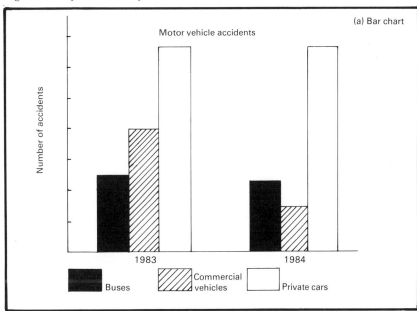

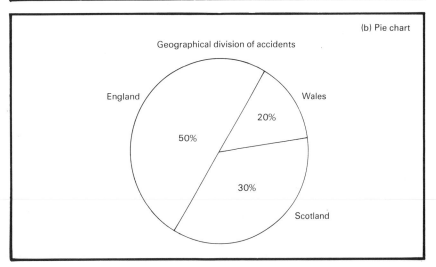

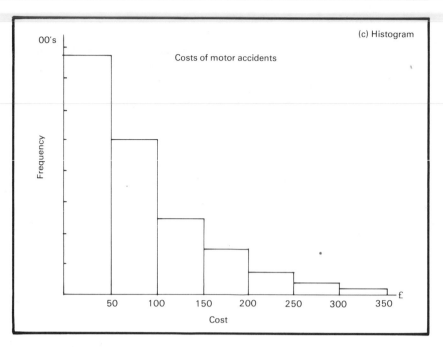

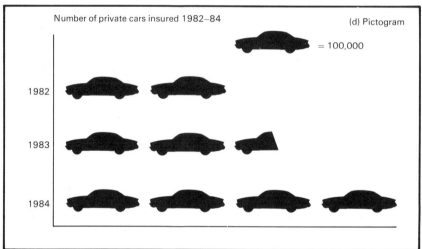

Diagram (a) is of a *bar chart* and you can see that two years, 1983 and 1984, are compared. The columns measure the number of accidents and at a glance it can be seen that the number of commercial vehicle incidents has reduced while the numbers of bus and private car accidents have remained almost the same.

The *pie chart* in diagram (b) shows the division of claims among the three geographical areas of England, Scotland and Wales. Each sector of the *pie* reflects the proportion of the total number of claims in that area, hence half of the *pie* represents 50 per cent of all claims.

In diagram (c) we have a *histogram* which measures the frequency with which some variable occurs. In this case we are measuring the frequency of claims costs. On the vertical axis we can see then that low cost claims are the most frequent and that very expensive claims occur much less frequently.

The final example is that of a *pictogram* which is a picture representation of a set of facts. This form of representing data is often seen in newspapers, on television and in company publicity brochures. Our *pictogram* shows the numbers of vehicles which an insurance company insures. Each car is equal to 100,000 vehicles insured and so from a start in 1982 of 200,000 cars we have increased to 250,000 and ultimately in 1984 to 400,000.

In addition to these methods of representing data, descriptive statistics also involves making certain measurements of data. The best known such measurement is the arithmetic mean. A company may describe its motor claims costs by saying that the average, or arithmetic mean, cost of such claims is £270. This describes the data and is helpful in a whole host of ways.

1D2B. Inferential statistics

This branch of statistics is possibly of more value to risk analysts. Descriptive statistics is historical in nature in the sense that it looks back and illustrates or describes what *has* happened. Inferential statistics takes this historical information and uses it to make inferences.

In our example of the motor risk the insurance company may want to collect information on the proportion of accidents which involved women drivers. It is unlikely that it would contact every person who had had an accident. It would be much more likely to gather information from a small group, a sample, and then make some inference about the whole group of accidents in the population.

This is a very common procedure not just in insurance but in many other walks of life. A medical equivalent is where the doctor takes a blood sample and on the basis of that sample is prepared to make some inference about your entire blood supply. An insurance company which takes a sample of claims and bases some inference upon that evidence, is doing exactly the same. Clearly this type of inference work is important in enabling a company to estimate the likely number and cost of claims and any other variable about the claim, such as age of person driving, number of passengers etc.

There is a range of additional statistical techniques available to insurers, all of which can be employed to assist the analysis of risk. Those students who progress to the final stages of the CII syllabus will study Quantitative Methods as Applied to Insurance, which takes these techniques much further than is either possible or appropriate in this present subject.

1D3. Probability theory

In analysing risk we were looking for a means of measuring our belief as to the likelihood of particular events. Probability theory represents one such measurement device.

Probabilities measure the likelihood that things will happen. They might be applied to measuring the likelihood of death at a certain age, a fire, earthquake, motor accident, plane crash or any number of risks.

Likelihood is measured on a scale from 0 to 1. Where it is absolutely certain to occur, the probability of it occurring is 1. It follows from this that an event with a probability of 0.2 is much less likely to occur than an event having a probability of 0.9.

Many people have put forward different scientific and philosophical arguments on the meaning of probability but for the purposes of this text we will highlight three views.

1D3A. A priori

When the total number of possible events is known we can compare this figure with the number of desired events and calculate an *a priori* probability.

In the real world it is unusual for the number of all possible events to be known and therefore the *a priori* concept has a limited application. It could be used, for example, in games of chance where we want to know the probability of getting a three on the roll of a dice. The total number of all possible events is six; we want only one of those six; the likelihood of getting the one we want is therefore one over six, or 0.1666.

1D3B. Relative frequency

One problem with measuring risk in a practical setting is that the total number of all possible outcomes is unknown. It is a bit like a football game. Before the game starts we do not know how many goals will be scored and after the game is over we only know how many were scored. We will never know how many goals were *not* scored.

It is the same with car accidents, explosions, fires or thefts. We will never know beforehand how many will occur or how severe they will be. We can look back over our past experience and base our measurement of likelihood on that. For example, we may operate a fleet of 1500 commercial vehicles and over the past years have averaged 50 accidents each year. We might use this experience to say that the probability of one of our vehicles having a collision next year is 50 divided by 1500, 0.0333. In other words, the probability of an accident occurring next year is equal to the relative frequency with which accidents have occurred in the past.

1D3C. Subjective probability

In certain cases there will be a total absence of past experience or at best very few occasions when the particular event has occurred. Such cases are not unknown to the world of insurance and often appear in headlines. Lloyd's of London, dealt with in chapter 5, has often received publicity when it has insured pianists' fingers, film stars' legs and other items for which no adequate statistical experience exists.

1D4. Psychological aspects

The measurement problem caused by the lack of past statistics is only one side of a very complex problem. Regardless of whether previous statistics are available there is one other very important aspect in the measurement of risk and that is the attitude which different people have to the same situation.

This can be shown easily by considering a gamble where one persons flips a coin. If the coin lands heads up he will pay you £10 but if it lands tails up you must pay him £5. Think about this very carefully and then ask others to do the same. It is unlikely that everyone you ask will agree to gamble. One factor that will affect our attitude is the amount of money we have to start with. The wealthy person may not mind gambling but if you only had £5 and you had promised to buy your wife a present with it you may dislike the gamble.

Take another brief example. Let us say that your friend has flipped a coin and has had twelve heads in a row, would you still gamble – remember you must pay him £5 if the next flip results in a tail? Based on so many heads in a row the 'chances' are that the next will be a tail and most would prefer not to gamble, but we had said earlier that the probability of getting a tail is 0.5, despite the numbers of previous flips there have been. This is an interesting finding as it tells us that even when probabilities exist to help us, we often assign our own measure of likelihood.

These two factors, our view of money based on our own wealth and our view of likelihood, represents the main psychological aspects of risk measurement and go a long way to explain the desire for insurance, as we shall see.

1D4A. Chance

Before leaving the question of risk measurement let us look at the use of the word 'chance'. This word often appears in the literature when risk is being discussed. People talk of the chance of something happening or some event coming about and we could have substituted 'chance' for 'uncertainty' in our definition of risk as the uncertainty of loss. There was, however, a good reason for not doing so and it is based on the occasions when people normally use the word 'chance'.

It would be unlikely for someone to talk about the risk of winning the football pools whereas it is quite normal for people to talk about the chance of winning the pools. In a similar way people normally refer to the risk of unemployment rather than the chance of unemployment. By monitoring when these two words are commonly used we can conclude that chance is reserved normally for those situations where the outcome is desired, e.g., winning the pools, and risk relates to outcomes that are not looked for e.g., the risk of being unemployed.

In this way it would be strange to talk of the chance of loss in the context of, say fire damage and more appropriate to refer to this as the risk of damage, or, as we have defined it, the uncertainty of loss.

1E. Conclusion

This first chapter has rarely mentioned insurance but has laid the foundation for much of what is to come later. It would be extremely difficult to learn about precious stones without ever looking at diamonds, or geology without examining rocks, or diseases without looking at patients. In the same way it would be impossible to understand insurance without looking at risk.

2. Insurance – A risk transfer mechanism

2A. How insurance works

In chapter 1 we examined the concept of risk from different points of view. We have established that both from a private and an industrial standpoint the existence of risk is important. The availability of insurance does not in itself cancel out risk. What insurance can do is to offer financial assistance to those who suffer the effects of risk. Hence a manufacturer with a £500,000 factory and £300,000 worth of machinery can effect insurance so that should that factory or machinery be damaged, say, by fire, he will receive some financial compensations.

It is in the interests of the community as a whole to have this manufacturer establish his business. By doing so he creates jobs, produces goods which people may need, and can provide work for suppliers of raw materials which in turn creates jobs, and so on. If the manufacturer sat down and thought about all the risks to which his factory and machinery could be exposed he may well decide simply to put the £800,000 in the bank and earn interest rather than have the bother and run the risk of establishing his business. Insurance, as we shall see, will be able to offer him some financial security which may then encourage him to continue with his business plans.

This idea of being able to insure raises all kinds of issues: what sort of risks can he insure, what will he be charged, how will claims be met, will a contract be necessary, what sort of conditions will have to be met, how will the cost of insurance be calculated, and so on. These technical aspects of insurance will only be touched on briefly in this book as other texts, for example *Principles and Practice of Insurance*, will deal with them more fully.

What we can say then is that a policy of insurance issued by an insurance company to the person insured will state what risks are covered by the policy, what the insurance cover will cost, the period of time over which the cover applies and other relevant matters. Having established these basic facts let us move on to examine in slightly more detail what the exact functions of insurance are.

2B. Primary function of insurance
2B1. Risk transfer

Insurance is a risk transfer mechanism, whereby the individual or the business enterprise can shift some of the uncertainty of life on to the shoulders of others. In return for a known premium, usually a very small amount compared with the potential loss, the cost of that loss can be transferred to an insurer. Without insurance, there would be a great deal of uncertainty experienced by an individual or an enterprise, not only as to whether a loss would occur, but also as to what size it would be if it did occur.

For example, a houseowner will realize that each year several hundred houses are damaged by fire. His uncertainty is whether in the coming year his house will be one of those damaged, and he is also uncertain, whether, given that he will be one of the unlucky ones, his loss will amount to a hundred pounds or so for the redecoration of his kitchen or whether the house will be gutted and cost him many thousands of pounds to repair.

Even though the probability of their house becoming one of the loss statistics is extremely low, most houseowners nevertheless elect to spend, say, £25–£30 on house insurance, rather than face the extremely remote possibility of losing a house worth £20,000.

In the case of business enterprises, the values exposed to loss are usually much higher, but in addition the hazards inherent in their operations are often higher than those of the houseowner, and so the premium charged is likely to be substantially higher than that for a house. Even in these circumstances the majority of firms prefer to pay a known cost of premium for the transfer of risk, rather than face the uncertainty of carrying the risk of loss.

2B2. The common pool

In the early days of marine insurance, the merchants agreed to make contributions to those suffering loss after the loss had taken place. This practice did not fully transfer the cost of uncertainty; it merely reduced it. A merchant undertaking a voyage would have the risk of a total loss removed from him, but the exact amount of his share of a loss could not be determined until after the event had taken place.

This state of affairs is not ideal and modern insurance practice fixes the insured's contributions (the premium) at the inception of the contract, so that he knows the full extent of his required share of losses for that year. It may, of course, vary in the light of the claims costs for future years.

The insured's premium is received by the insurer into a fund or pool for that type of risk, and the claims of those suffering losses are paid out of this pool. An insurance company will pay its motor claims out of the monies it has received from those insuring motor cars, and so on.

Because of the large number of clients in any particular fund or pool, the insurance company can predict with reasonable accuracy the amount of claims likely to be incurred in the coming year. There will be some variation in claims costs from year to year and the premiums include a small margin to build up a reserve upon which the company can draw in bad years. Therefore, subject to the limitations of the type of cover bought, the insured will not be required to make further contributions to the common pool after the loss.

2B3. Equitable premiums

Assuming that a risk transfer mechanism has been set up through a common fund or pool, the third primary function is that the contributions paid into the fund should be fair to all the parties participating.

Each party wishing to insure will bring to the fund differing degrees of risk of loss to the fund. For example, a timber built house presents a different hazard from one of standard brick construction; an 18-year-old driver is more hazardous than one aged 35; two 35-year-old drivers, one with a family saloon and one with a high powered sports car, present different hazards; someone grossly overweight has a higher chance of early death than a person of average weight; a factory worker is likely to have a higher risk of injury than an office worker; the man with a house worth £50,000 has a potentially larger claim on the fund than one with a house worth £25,000.

These examples could be summarized under two main headings, hazard and value, and in aggregate the contributions to the fund must be sufficient to meet the total cost of claims brought about by these factors. In addition, there will be the costs of administering the fund and of creating reserves to ensure that abnormally heavy claims in future years can still be met, and an allowance for a margin of profit to the insurers in their operations.

Factors such as these must be taken into account by the underwriter, i.e., the person accepting the proposal on behalf of the insurers. In fixing the level of premium for each case he must try to ensure that the level of contribution made to the fund by a particular policyholder is equitable compared with the contributions of others, bearing in mind the likely frequency and severity of claims which may be made by that policyholder. Finally, the level of premium fixed must be relatively competitive, otherwise the insurer will go out of business due to lack of new orders.

To summarize, the primary function of insurance is to provide a risk transfer mechanism by means of a common pool into which each policyholder pays a fair and equitable premium, according to the risk of loss he or she brings to the pool.

2C. Subsidiary functions
2C1. Stimulus to business enterprise

The main stimulus to enterprise is the release of funds for investment in the productive side of a business, which would require to be held in easily accessible reserves if the firm had not transferred the risk to an insurer. The medium and large sized firms would probably create reserve funds for emergencies which might put their whole future viability in jeopardy. While these funds could be invested, it would be imprudent to invest any sizeable part of them in the business and the rate of return which could be obtained externally for quickly realizable investments would be less than if the money were available for internal investment. The premium payable to an insurer would only be a small proportion of the fund required because of the pooling arrangements, and so most of this money could be invested in new plant, buildings or stock.

2C1A. Security

In the small firm, the security from loss which insurance provides means that losses which would be crippling to the small firm, although insignificant to the larger firm, can now be faced with confidence. Even in the larger firm, the executives can concentrate on the proper function of running an efficient enterprise. They can concentrate on the production and trading risks without the worry that the objectives in these fields may not be achieved due to fire or other insurable risk.

A healthy and vigorous economy usually has available to it a well organized insurance market. The American writers Mehr and Cammack observe (*Principles of Insurance* 1976) that the rise of Britain as a great trading nation and the fact that we had exceptionally sound fire insurance facilities at the same period, was no coincidence.

Several writers are of the opinion that insurance helps to bring about a closer approach to an optimum allocation of the factors of production and hence optimum price levels.

Frequently those wishing to invest in new projects will only do so if the maintenance of adequate insurance cover is written into the construction contract.

International trade is stimulated also, as a marine cargo policy is one of the documents which, along with a letter of credit, bill of lading, bill of exchange and export invoice, is essential to enable the seller of goods to ask his bank to discount the bill of exchange and so obtain funds immediately, instead of having funds tied up in cargo on the high seas.

2C2. Loss prevention

Fire surveyors are trained to identify sources of potential risk in the production process, storage of materials and use of electricity, etc. They make recommendations which will limit the incidence of loss from these sources to a minimum.

Theft surveyors make recommendations for the protection of property against thieves. The protective devices installed on their recommendation will deter many casual thieves, again reducing the number of losses.

In a similar manner, the liability surveyor will endeavour to advise the businessman or employer in ways to prevent claims from the public, due to their operations or products, or from employees, due to unsafe conditions of work.

Ideally, these experts should be consulted at the planning stage of a project, but as yet too few architects and planners realize the valuable help which is available to them and their clients. The recommendations will require to be incorporated into the building or plant at a later date in any event, and it is much less costly to have the loss prevention measures incorporated at the building stage. Pressure and lifting plant and ships are required by statute to be inspected by competent engineers and these people are often employed by insurance companies. These types of plant are usually inspected during construction and again at frequent intervals during their lifetime.

2C2A. Research and liaison

Insurers actively contribute to research into the prevention of loss and liaise with various public and private bodies in this connection. Insurers' organisations such as FIRTO, FOC and BIA are discussed in detail in chapter 5.

2C3. Loss control

The various surveyors mentioned above are concerned not only with preventing loss (which can never be achieved fully due to human limitations), but also with the limitation or control of losses which do occur. For example, the Fire Offices' Committee lays down rules and regulations as to the construction of buildings, design of fire doors, sprinkler installations, and alarm systems, so that fires which do start may be contained for sufficient time to enable the public fire service to get to the scene and extinguish the blaze before it becomes a major disaster.

Similarly the theft surveyor is aware that he cannot prevent the determined criminal from entering a building, but he can make it a difficult, time consuming, and noisy process so that the quantity of material stolen may be limited.

2C3A. Salvage corps

Until March 1984 insurers in Glasgow, Liverpool and London maintained an organization known as the Salvage Corps. The function of the Salvage Corps, which operated on very similar lines to those of the fire service, was to attend fires and reduce losses flowing from the fire; often the cost of smoke and water damage far exceeds the value of the goods actually destroyed in the fire. The Salvage Corps were frequently able to take steps to minimize the damage to goods and property and played a large part in post-fire salvage operations. However, the insurance industry decided it could no longer afford to maintain this force and it has now been disbanded.

2C3B. Loss adjusters

The investigation of losses, their causes and the values involved, is often a highly technical process which requires very quick action after the loss in order to assess these factors accurately and to take steps to minimize further loss.

It would be uneconomic for insurers to have teams of experts in various fields scattered around the country, as many of them would be under-employed for much of the time. This problem has been overcome by independent firms of loss adjusters setting up offices in the larger towns and cities, and providing these services, on a fee basis, to the insurers in the locality. These experts contribute greatly to the limitation of the cost of loss, by knowing how best to get a business on its feet again quickly, where to purchase or hire temporary plant, where to dispose of salvage at the best price, and so on.

2C4. Social benefits

In chapter 1 we itemized the cost of a number of different forms of risk and clearly there is some social benefit to be derived from a system which will share losses.

The fact that a factory owner has adequate fire insurance cover means that he has the capital to reinstate his factory and so recreate jobs for his workers, who might otherwise be unemployed for a considerable time. Frequently several firms in an area are dependent on other firms, either as customers or as suppliers and so they too may be at risk. When the multiplier effect of the reduced income of a group of workers is taken into account, society at large in that locality may suffer if a firm goes into liquidation after an uninsured loss. If full consequential loss (loss of profits) insurance has been arranged in addition to the material loss cover, there may not be the need for even temporary lay-offs of workers following a major loss.

The aid which insurance provides in maintaining industry in an area stabilizes the economy of that area and in aggregate helps to stabilize the national economy through the continued sources of rates and taxes.

We enjoy, in this country, the benefits of comprehensive welfare payments from the State, but these are sometimes limited in amount (e.g., death benefits, widow's and old age pensions) (see chapter 9). The individual can purchase, through life assurance, income benefits and lump sums for dependants, and many employers provide group life assurance, pension benefits and disablement schemes for their employees, thus supplementing the State benefits. Without these benefits being available from the insurance market, either the State benefits would require to be increased for a much wider range of people than at present or many more of our sick, aged and bereaved would be impoverished.

2C5. Savings

Another benefit which stems from the provision of life assurance cover, is the use of endowment assurances as a means of saving. The most frequent uses of these contracts are in saving a lump sum for retirement, in conjunction with a house purchase mortgage or for children's education or majority. As these contracts are long term ones the temptation to end the contract early has financial penalties by way of surrender values below the value paid in. The saver is therefore more inclined to keep on paying the premium, compared with saving in a bank or building society.

2D. Associated functions

When a risk transfer system is set up there are certain functions evolving from those operations which are not the direct result of the desire to transfer risk or obtain benefits for society. Insurers, as custodians of the premiums paid, invest these funds so that they are available when required, be it within the next 12 months in the case of property claims, the next two or three years in the case of liability claims or in anything up to forty or fifty years in the case of life assurance. Since London is the main insurance centre of the world the transactions of British insurers extend beyond our shores, and when they are carrying foreign risks there is a flow of overseas earnings or, as they are normally called, invisible earnings, into Britain to help our balance of payments. This point is referred to later in this chapter and in chapter 8.

2D1. Investment of funds

As indicated above, when an insurance premium is received into the fund, any likely claims will arise some time in the future, from a few weeks or months to several years. The insurers must try to obtain the best overall return on the investment of these funds, that is, a mixture of high interest rates and the highest capital appreciation, in order to keep pace with inflation and to increase profits.

The money is not left in bank vaults for various reasons but mainly because a wide spread of different types of investment is desirable for safety reasons, and very often better returns are obtained elsewhere. By making this spread of investments the insurance market helps national and local governments in their short and medium term borrowings, and industry and commerce by various kinds of loans and the provision of working capital by taking up share issues. Life and pension funds may be invested in property owned by the insurers or in which they have a major interest and leased to various commercial interests. This latter type of investment has proved to be excellent for capital appreciation over the years and provides an income each year by way of rents. A summary of these investments is given below for 1982.

	Long-term funds £m	General funds £m
British government authority securities	21,681	3,777
Foreign and Commonwealth government provincial and municipal stocks	2,739	3,709
Debentures, loan stocks preference and guaranteed stocks and shares	3,734	2,957
Ordinary stocks and shares	28,065	5,100
Mortgages	5,100	742
Real property and ground rents	17,267	2,041
Other investments	3,461	1,757
	82,047	20,083

Source: BIA Facts and Figures

2D2.Invisible earnings

We have already mentioned the fact that insurance allows people to spread risk among themselves. In the same way we can also say that countries spread risk. A great deal of insurance is transacted in the UK in respect of property and liabilities incurred overseas. London is very much the centre of world insurance and large volumes of insurance premium flow in every year. This activity is described as *invisible earnings*, and is similar to the exporting of goods. In the latter case a visible trade exists and goods are shipped to some foreign country and then paid for by that country. This is a form of visible export from which we earn money. As a trading island nation we have to import many different types of goods which we need; in turn we export things which we have or make which other countries want. This trading produces a balance in the sense that we either export more than we import or import more than we export. Clearly, from an economic point of view it would be better to export more than we import as then we would have a net inflow of money, or as we call it, a surplus, on our 'Balance of Trade'. In recent years, as a result of being able to export oil, we have had such a surplus. However, before the oil was discovered, and possibly when it runs out, we shall be back in the position of having a deficit on our Balance of Trade, i.e. of importing more than we export.

We have described only *visible* trade so far. There is also the trading in *invisible* goods such as banking, tourism and, most importantly for us, insurance. These invisible exports have earned Britain vast sums of money over the years and in many cases have been enough to wipe out the deficit on the *visible* trading. In chapter 8 we discuss the role of these invisible earnings in a little more detail, suffice to say here that in 1982 insurance companies, Lloyd's and insurance brokers had invisible earnings of £1174m. This is not the total of the premiums which flowed in from overseas, (this figure was £20,518m), but the amount which was *earned* after claims and expenses had been met. The net invisible earnings of £1174m represented 27 per cent of the invisible earnings of all UK financial institutions, as can be seen from figure 2/1.

Figure 2/1 Earnings of UK Financial Institutions 1982

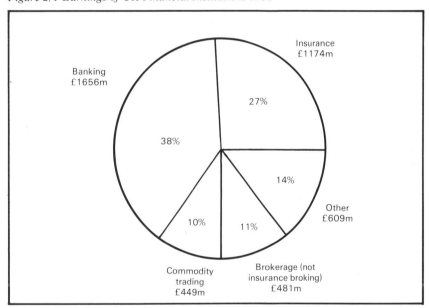

Source: BIA Facts and Figures

We have seen that in providing for the primary function of transfer of risk, by equitable contribution to a common fund, various other functions are performed.

The security given by risk transfer acts as an often unnoticed stimulus to commercial and industrial activity. The efforts of insurers in loss prevention and loss reduction mean that industrial effort can create new capital, rather than replace some of the capital which would be destroyed otherwise.

Finally, insurance is an international operation, with London still the leading centre of activity. This has meant that Britain usually leads the world in providing cover, and in the process earns millions of pounds in overseas earnings.

The international role of insurance is examined in more detail in chapter 8.

2E.Insurable risks

So far we have introduced the idea of risk and the need to seek financial protection. We have outlined the way in which insurance satisfies this need for protection and have looked at the primary, subsidiary and associated functions of insurance.

What we must do now is to consolidate what we know. Clearly it cannot be possible to give insurance protection for all risky events. For example, it would not be right for an insurance company to pay for fire damage which you have deliberately caused to your own property, nor would it seem just for you to insure your neighbour's house so that you could collect some financial compensation if it were damaged. For these and other reasons we have to place some restriction on the risks which are insurable.

Rather than create a list of the kinds of events which can or cannot be insured, if such a list could ever be compiled, we have selected another approach. Still fixing our attention on risk itself we will explore the characteristics of the insurable risk. Insurable risks have certain common features including those shown in figure 2/2 and discussed below.

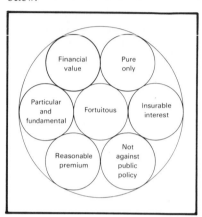

Figure 2/2 Common features of insurable risks

2E1.Financial value

The risk must involve a loss that is capable of financial measurement. We have touched on this before and it is important to remember that insurance is concerned only with situations where monetary compensation is given following a loss. This feature of the insurable risk is easily identified in, for example, damage to property where the level of compensation can be equated with the cost of repairs.

Where property is stolen it is similarly easy to measure the loss in financial terms. Where someone is injured by you in, for example, a motor car accident, then the court will decide how much the injured person should receive in compensation. This amount is then a financial measure of your risk.

In the vast majority of cases the financial value of the risk will not be known before the event occurs but all we are concerned with is that when it does take place the loss is capable of financial measurement.

In life assurance it is rather more difficult to say that the financial loss suffered by a wife when her husband dies is a specific sum of money. What we can say is that the level of compensation to be paid in the event of death has been determined prior to taking out the policy.

2E2.Homogeneous exposures

There must be a large number of similar, homogeneous, risks before any one of that number is capable of being insured. There are two reasons for this. The first is that, as we have noted already, the measurement of risk by probabilities and statistics relies on there being a reasonable experience of past events. Statistics have been compiled by most insurance companies on common risks such as fires, explosions, motor accidents, thefts, injuries and deaths. One minor exception to this criterion was mentioned in chapter 1 when we discussed subjective probabilities and the insurance of certain unique and unusual occurrences.

The second is that if there were only three or four exposures then each one would have to contribute a very high amount if losses were to be met from these contributions. On the other hand if there were thousands of similar exposures then the contributions could be comparatively small as only a few would be unfortunate enough to suffer a loss and hence require it to be met from the contributions. The insurance of household contents against fire is an example of homogeneous exposures, whereas the insuring of a concert pianist's fingers is not.

2E3.Pure risks only

Insurance is concerned only with pure risks; speculative risks, where there is the possibility of some gain, cannot be insured. This is generally the case although certain modern developments may lead us to alter this statement in due course. Speculative risks are normally taken in the hope of a gain and the provision of insurance may act as a distinct disincentive to effort in that even if you do not try as hard as you could to bring about the gain you will still earn the profit from your insurance policy. This is obviously not acceptable but in addition the speculative risk can often be unacceptable for other reasons such as lack of statistical experience or high probability of a loss on the part of the insurer.

It is important to note we are not concluding that all pure risks are insurable; what we are saying is that speculative risks, on the whole, are not.

2E4. Particular and fundamental risks

Particular risks are generally insurable provided they satisfy the other criteria of insurable risks. Fundamental risks however do not present such a straightforward picture.

The widespread, indiscriminate nature of the effect of most fundamental risks has resulted in them, traditionally, being uninsurable. It is not accurate to say that all fundamental risks cannot be insured but it is true to say that insurers are very careful in selecting those for which they wish to provide cover.

Fundamental risks that arise out of the nature of the society we live in are largely uninsurable and those that arise due to some physical occurrence depend for their insurability on the circumstances.

As a result, war and changing customs are largely uninsurable. Fundamental risks due to some physical occurrence such as climatic or tidal conditions may be insurable but this could depend, for example, on the geographical location of the object being insured.

2E5. Fortuitous

The loss must be entirely fortuitous as far as the person seeking insurance is concerned. It is not possible to insure against an event that will occur with certainty as in such a case there would be no risk, no uncertainty of loss. The frequency and severity of any risk must be completely beyond the control of the person insuring.

In the case of most risks this will always be apparent but in life assurance some could argue that there is no uncertainty about death; it is one of the few certainties we have. Life assurances is however still involved with fortuitous events as it is the timing of death that is beyond the control of the person effecting the policy. This is not true in the case of suicide and most policies will cover death from suicide as long as it occurs a reasonable time after the policy was taken out, i.e., suicide was not being planned, at least not in the short term, when the policy was effected.

2E6. Insurable interest

The risk that is to be insured must result in some form of financial loss, and it is easy to anticipate situations where a person could insure some other person's house or car so that when the house or car was damaged he, in addition to the owner of the property, would receive compensation from the insurance company. To take this thought a stage further, there would be no reason why a person could not go round to the local hospital and take out a life assurance policy on the lives of those people who were very ill.

To counteract this possibility one of the basic doctrines of insurance is that the person insuring must be the one who stands to suffer some financial loss if the risk materializes. This topic is discussed at length in the CII tuition course 040 *Principles and practice of insurance*.

2E7. Against public policy

It is a common principle in law that contracts must not be contrary to what society considers the right and moral thing to do. This applies to insurance contracts in the same way and one form of risk that is not insurable is one that is against public policy. It would not be acceptable to society at large if a person could burn down his own factory or shop in order to recover insurance money and this form of risk has been catered for above when we said that the loss must be fortuitous as far as the person insuring is concerned.

One form of risk that was not mentioned earlier was the risk of being fined by the police. The fine is intended to penalize the person and while insurance may be available to meet the losses following, say, a motor accident it is not possible to provide insurance to pay the fine of the driver who was found guilty of some offence.

2E8. Reasonable premium

The final feature of the insurable risk is that the premium must be seen to be reasonable in relation to the likely financial loss. A risk that results in a loss with an extremely high frequency may involve a premium that would be unreasonable from the insuring person's point of view. Similarly a straightforward risk such as that caused by fire or theft may result in an unreasonable premium, depending upon the object exposed. The insurance premium required to cover a ball point pen against fire or theft may be quite unreasonable in relation to the potential financial loss in view of the insurance company's costs.

2F. Conclusion

The existence of these characteristics should be looked for in any risk against which insurance is sought. The criteria outlined above obviously place some limit on the range of risks which can be insured but this should not be over-emphasised. The whole network of insurance which we now go on to examine has grown and developed in the face of these limitations. Those common features protect insurance companies and it may be that adherence to them has played a large part in building a strong insurance market place.

References
Steele, J. T., *Principles and practice of insurance*. CII Tuition Service London 1984.

3. Insurance through the ages

3A.Importance of history

The concept of insurance is not new. A form of insurance even existed in early Rome where Romans gathered together in burial societies. They all contributed to a fund and the members of the pool had their burial costs met by the society. This was an early forerunner of the common pool, discussed in the previous chapter.

To examine the origin of modern insurance is a fascinating area of study in itself. It can, however, also be valuable to those who are embarking upon the study of insurance as it exists today. A knowledge of the origins of a subject is always beneficial, and for insurance we can identify at least three reasons why it is important to look back.

Firstly, many of our modern insurance institutions, such as Lloyd's of London, would be extremely difficult to understand if we did not enquire into their history. Secondly, insurance companies and Lloyd's have perfected the method of practising insurance over many years and a large part of present-day practice, including certain policy wordings, would prove quite inexplicable if we had no knowledge of their development. Finally, insurance has often been a response to some problem faced by society and an understanding of how insurance companies faced up to and solved important issues goes a long way to explaining many present-day methods.

Figure 3/1. Development of insurance

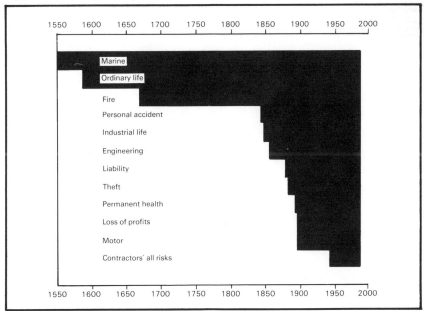

Figure 3/1 shows the chronological development of twelve of the more common forms of insurance. Chapter 4 will look at the present classes of insurance, including those in figure 3/1. In the meantime we will look at the historical development of these twelve forms and some others. Rather than treat each form of insurance independently we will group them into four main divisions as follows: marine and aviation, loss or damage to property, life and health, and liability and financial. There is no significance to these divisions other than that they represent convenient headings under which to study the development of several different forms of insurance. In the meantime it is interesting to note from figure 3/1 the expansion in the forms of cover available in the post-industrial revolution years.

3B. Marine and aviation

Since earliest times man has been fascinated by sea travel and preoccupied with thoughts of air travel. It is not unusual, therefore, that man's first attempt at seeking protection was from the danger posed by the sea. Historians have uncovered evidence suggesting that some sharing of losses did exist among seafarers as early as the ninth century BC. In contrast, aviation insurance is of far more recent origin.

3B1. Marine insurance development

Lloyd's is probably the most famous insurance market in the world, being the centre for the world's marine insurance and shipping intelligence.

In the 17th century insurance of ships and cargoes was often underwritten by merchants who were willing to carry part of the risk of a voyage for part of the premium. Commerce of various types was transacted among the merchants who met each other in the various coffee houses around the City of London. Similarly, those wishing to transact insurance would meet in these coffee houses. One of them, owned by one Edward Lloyd, was situated near the River Thames and was frequented by merchants, shipowners and others having an interest in maritime ventures.

Lloyd's Coffee House was situated in Tower Street and was in existence by 1688, although the original date of opening is uncertain. Edward Lloyd encouraged the merchants or underwriters (they signed their names at the foot of the insurance contracts) because it brought extra business to his coffee house. He supplied shipping information and published a news sheet in 1696, called 'Lloyd's News'. This was superseded some years after his death by 'Lloyd's List' which is London's oldest newspaper.

In 1769 the insurance market transferred its business centre to the 'New Lloyd's Coffee House' in Pope's Head Alley and in 1771 a Committee was formed to seek larger premises. With their membership subscriptions premises were established in 1774 in the Royal Exchange.

The formation of the Committee took the running of Lloyd's out of the hands of the coffee house owner (now Thomas Fielding) and into the hands of the insurance fraternity.

The modern Corporation of Lloyd's was formed in 1871 by Act of Parliament and more recent statutes have kept the constitution up to date with the needs of a modern insurance market. The present premises are centred in Lime Street, London.

London is now the world centre of marine insurance and it is interesting that its introduction to Britain was by the Lombards, merchants from Northern Italy in the 13th, 14th and 15th centuries. The practice of marine insurance grew quite considerably in these centuries and by 1575 the need was felt for some formalisation of the provision of marine policies; the Chamber of Assurances was therefore established whereby every policy had to be registered. The effect of the Chamber was the introduction of a standardised policy, which has survived almost unaltered to this day, and a reduction in the number of disputes arising over cover and the existence of policies. Finally it gave an air of formality and permanence to marine insurance that had been lacking. Twenty-six years later, in 1601, the Court of Arbitration was established to consider disputes on marine policies and it met in the Chamber of Assurances.

3B1A. Chartered companies monopoly

In 1720 the London Assurance and the Royal Exchange Assurance were granted Royal Charters to transact marine insurance. The Act providing for the incorporation of the two companies, the Bubble Act, also restricted the provision of marine insurance to these two companies or to individuals. In other words the two companies had almost gained a monopoly as only they or individuals could provide marine insurance. Not unnaturally, to achieve this privileged position some amount of backroom work was necessary, culminating in what some historians refer to as bribery, when both companies offered £300,000 for their charter to the King, who was much in need of money at the time.

As only individuals could provide marine insurance it is little wonder that the activities in Edward Lloyd's coffee house prospered and, as we will find in chapter 5, Lloyd's has developed as a market place for insurance provided by individuals.

The monopoly was terminated eventually in 1824 when the Alliance Marine Insurance Company was successful in an application to provide marine insurance.

3B1B. Marine Insurance Act 1906

The case law that was being accumulated over the years, some 2,000 cases, was incorporated in the Marine Insurance Act of 1906 when the law relating to marine insurance was codified, that is, brought together in the one statute. The Act forms the basis for the operation of marine insurance to this day and a knowledge of its terms is essential to anyone embarking upon a career in marine insurance. Its value goes beyond the boundary of marine insurance as it is the only code of commercial insurance on the statute book and for that reason is of considerable importance in its own right.

3B2. Aviation insurance development

The development of aviation insurance is rather easier to record in view of its comparatively recent origins. As with the motor car it was the First World War that highlighted the value of planes and air transport. In 1919 the first regular civil aviation service started but it was not until 1923 that the British Aviation Insurance Group, representing a group formed by the Union of Canton Insurance Company and the White Cross Insurance Company, began offering aviation insurance. This group changed its name twice and by 1936 was known as the Aviation and General Insurance Co. Ltd. Lloyd's syndicates played a major role in the provision of aviation insurance and much of the business is placed with them.

3C. Loss or damage to property

It has always been possible for people to take physical steps in order to safeguard property from damage or loss. As communities grew and people came together to live in towns and villages there arose a greater dependency on each other. This dependency gave rise to the desire for some form of financial protection and records do show that for fire damage at least, this need was met in a crude manner after losses were incurred. This financial help was paid for from donations and the schemes were normally organised by local guilds of craftsmen or churches. A far more formal means of providing compensation was, however, necessary and following the Great Fire of London in 1666 several developments took place.

3C1. Fire insurance development
3C1A. Early fire insurance companies

Some early documents provide evidence of the existence of fire insurance in 1667, but the Fire Office is generally regarded as being the first fire insurance company, set up in 1680. The Fire Office later, in 1705, changed its name to the Phenix as this was the symbol represented on the company's fire mark. These fire marks, normally made of metal, bore the insignia of the fire insurance company and were nailed to an outside wall. They performed two very valuable functions. The first was that they were a cheap and prominent form of advertising and the second, of more importance to the owner of the property and thereby providing the incentive to display them, was that they indicated to the fire brigade that the house was insured. It has to be remembered that fire brigades were controlled by, mainly, the insurance companies and each ran independently. It was important, therefore, to display the fire marks so as to guide the fire brigade to the insured building. Following an abortive attempt at municipal insurance by the Corporation of London during the period 1681–1682 a second company, the Friendly Society, was founded in 1683.

The third office, appropriately titled The Amicable Contributors for insuring houses from loss by Fire, came along in 1696 and soon became known as the Hand-in-Hand. It transacted business successfully until 1905 when it was absorbed by the Commercial Union.

Later companies were the Sun Fire Office, 1710, the Union, 1714, and the Westminster, 1717.

3C1B. Growth in fire insurance

The Industrial Revolution changed the face of the British industrial scene and engendered many more items which needed to be insured. Large new factories were built, housing complicated machinery; volumes of goods were processed by these factories and transported to warehouses, moved around the country and shipped overseas.

This mushrooming of industrial activity did, of course, bring with it a growth in the demand for fire insurance protection. By the beginning of the nineteenth century there were very many insurance companies transacting fire insurance but there was little contact between them.

Associated action was nevertheless felt to be desirable for, at least, two reasons. A large number of properties being insured were similar and needless competition could be avoided if there was some pooling of experience so that risks could be classified in a common manner and rates formulated. Secondly there was some need for concerted action in fighting fires and effort in this direction, if it was to come at all, would probably be instigated by the fire insurers.

Some headway on the fire fighting was made in 1832 when the London fire offices formed a fire brigade instead of each running their own. The question of agreement on classification of risks and common rates was more difficult to resolve. The Scottish fire office managers led the way in 1829 but in England associated action tended to be on a geographical basis. It was not until 1860 that one association was formed with separate committees meeting in Scotland, London and Liverpool or Manchester. In 1868 this association formalised a constitution and became known as the Fire Offices' Committee. More on the work of the FOC will be given in chapter 5.

3C1C.Tooley Street fire

On 22 June 1861 one of the landmarks in the development of fire insurance took place. A fire broke out in wharves and warehouses along the banks of the Thames near to the centre of London. The fire spread quickly and caused damage costing the fire insurance companies, in aggregate, £1,000,000.

The immediate response was a large increase in premiums charged for this type of property but after representations from city merchants they were modified. What resulted from the Tooley Street fire was:

(a) the problems of how much to charge for wharves and warehouses was dealt with by a new committee, The London Wharf and Warehouse Committee;

(b) differential rates of charges were adopted in an effort to encourage owners to think about fire precautions. Bad features were penalized and good ones rewarded;

(c) the inadequacy of the existing fire fighting forces was highlighted and the Metropolitan Fire Brigade Act 1865 established a fire service for London run by the city itself;

(d) two new companies were formed, the Commercial Union and the Mercantile, later the North British and Mercantile.

3C2.Non-fire loss or damage

So far we have concentrated on fire damage but fire is by no means the only risk to which early industrialists were exposed. It was soon found necessary to add to fire policies a range of additional perils such as storm, flood, burst pipes and others.

3C2A.Theft insurance

One of the other most common forms of loss involving property is theft but it was not until 1887 that the first fire policy was extended to include theft cover. The Mercantile Accident and Guarantee Insurance Company began issuing theft policies in 1889, although the term used then was burglary. The use of the word theft followed on from the Theft Act 1968 when the legal definition of what constituted a theft was given. The Fine Art and General Insurance Company Ltd., in 1890, the Goldsmiths and General Burglary Insurance Association in 1891 and the National Burglary Insurance Corporation in 1892 continued the development of theft insurance as a separate form of business.

Towards the end of the nineteenth century a logical development of fire and theft insurance came about with the introduction of all risks covers. This form of insurance represented a wide form of cover against loss of or damage to property from almost any cause, subject to certain exceptions. This therefore includes fire, theft and other forms of accidental damage.

In the following chapter we will see how all risks insurance has extended to include such covers as goods-in-transit, loss of money and damage to construction work.

3C2B.Engineering

The changes brought about by the Industrial Revolution brought with them many problems. One such problem was posed by the risk of damage and injury inherent in the operation of new machinery. The most frequent occurrence in connection with machinery was the explosion of boilers and other pressure plant that was then being employed to power machinery.

Safety standards were little thought of in these early days and it is interesting to note that the development of engineering insurance ran in parallel with the safety inspection of boilers. In 1854 the Steam Boiler Assurance Company began issuing insurance policies combined with an inspection service. Eventually public feeling grew to such an extent that in 1882 the Boiler Explosions Act was passed, by which severe penalties could be imposed if the explosion of a boiler was found to have been the fault of the owner. This form of legislation continued and expanded to cover other areas of industrial health and safety and we shall look at some of it later.

3D.Life, personal accident and health

We commented earlier on the existence of burial societies in the ancient world. This form of activity continued but it did not take account of the dependants who were left nor did it provide any compensation to a person who was injured but not fatally.

3D1.Ordinary life assurance

It is in the year 1583 that we have the first real evidence, in Britain, of life assurance as we know it today.

A policy was taken out on 18 June 1583 on the life of William Gibbons for a sum of £382.6s.8d (£382.33). The contract was for twelve months and the money was to be paid if Gibbons died within the year. He did, in fact, die on 8th May 1584 and after a slight dispute over whether twelve months meant twelve times 28 days or twelve calendar months, the money was paid.

The short term form of policy taken out by William Gibbons was typical of the type of assurance issued in these early days. The provision of life assurance continued almost unaltered for the next century with the short term form of policy mentioned above, and a form of mutual association, similar in design to the ancient burial societies, where members contributed to a common fund out of which payments were made on the death of members.

3D1A. Mutual associations

One such mutual association that grew in prosperity was the Amicable Society for a Perpetual Assurance Office founded in 1705 by Royal Charter. The significance of the charter will become clear in chapter 5 when we examine the formation of insurance companies. The 'Amicable' transacted business on traditional lines but in 1757 they took the daring step of guaranteeing a minimum sum to be payable in the event of death. This seemed to satisfy a demand as the company did not suffer by its boldness.

3D1B. Actuarial principles

Around the turn of the century at roughly the same time as the 'Amicable' was founded, mathematicians were working on what have become known as mortality tables. Two of the most important contributions were by Edmund Halley, the astronomer in 1693, after whom Halley's comet is named, and James Dodson, then mathematics master at the school attached to Christ's Hospital, in 1755. The intention of the mortality tables was, in part, to be able to state in mathematical terms the likelihood of persons of a given age dying. The objective they aimed at is well described by Halley when he wrote '. . . that the price of insurance on lives might be regulated by the age of the persons on whose life the insurance is made.' Dodson followed this idea and on being refused assurance by the Amicable on account of his age, '. . . determined to form a new society on a plan of assurance on more equitable terms than those of the Amicable, which takes the same premium for all ages'.

He did not have to wait long. In 1762 the Equitable Life Assurance Society was formed and transacted business on the basis suggested by him. They were able to offer life assurance on level premiums that were dependent upon the age of the person when he took out the policy. This was a significant difference from previous companies. In addition they offered a whole life policy that paid the sum assured on the death of the assured person. This was possible as the work of Dodson and others had introduced an element of science into the business of knowing how much to charge. This science is now known as actuarial science and is taught at many universities and colleges; examinations are conducted by the Faculty of Actuaries in Scotland and Institute of Actuaries in England. Much of what we now know as actuarial mathematics is built upon the early work of Richard Price and his nephew William Morgan who were both associated with the 'Equitable', Morgan as actuary for more than fifty years.

3D1C. Life Assurance Act 1774

The next landmark in the development was the passing of the Life Assurance Act 1774 the title of which explains its purpose, 'An act for regulating insurances upon lives and prohibiting all such insurances except in cases where persons insuring shall have an interest on the life or death of the person insured'.

By the end of the eighteenth century several proprietary companies (see chapter 5) had been formed where policyholders did not share in profits – as they had with mutual associations. These proprietary companies were spearheaded by the Westminster Society, 1792, and the Pelican Life Office, 1797.

3D2. Industrial life assurance

What we have described so far has been the development of what is now known as ordinary life assurance. This is to be contrasted with industrial life assurance. The changing structure of society brought about by the Industrial Revolution produced the beginnings of the 'industrial' classes. The men and women who worked in the new industries were not financially protected against infirmity and the onset of old age as employees are today, and in order to avoid the stigma of the poor laws many friendly societies were formed. These societies, thousands of which were in existence before the end of the eighteenth century, allowed some provision for sickness and funeral expenses. Out of the friendly solciety grew the concept of industrial life assurance, with companies transacting life assurance that was especially suited to the needs and pockets of the 'industrial' classes.

3D3. Personal accident and health insurance

What a change it must have been during the Industrial Revolution for a predominantly agricultural people to be confronted by the then new machinery of the day. One of the most breath-taking sights must have been that of the early railway locomotives thundering across the countryside.

These early trains were not very safe and in addition to the fire risk caused by flying sparks there was also a high probability of accidents. In 1848 the Railway Passengers Assurance Company began offering policies aimed at providing compensation in the event of an accident. The idea of personal accident insurance grew, and two years later in 1850 the Accidental Death Indemnity Company issued policies providing benefit for death from any cause for a premium of £1 for every £1000 insured. This company went a stage further and introduced compensation for non-fatal accidents as well as cover for medical charges during any period of disability.

The next major development came when in 1885, the Edinburgh-based company, Sickness and Accident Insurance Association, started issuing policies that provided for compensation payments in the event of certain specified sicknesses.

3D3A. Permanent health

One serious drawback to these forms of cover is that once a person contracts an illness or disease the insurer is unlikely to renew the policy once the twelve months insurance year has expired. To overcome this problem a form of 'permanent' cover was developed, now commonly referred to as permanent health insurance. The prospective insured is medically examined and, if found suitable, a policy is issued which continues in force until a specified age, normally retiral age. The policy cannot be cancelled by the insurer, irrespective of the insured's state of health, and compensation continues to be paid as long as the disablement lasts or until the insured reaches the specified age. This form of cover is particularly suitable for self-employed people who may lose income or incur additional expense when they are sick.

3E. Liability and financial insurances

This category comprises those risks where the loss suffered by the person insuring is either an amount of money he is to pay as compensation to another or some loss of his own money.

3E1. Liability insurance development

The development of liability insurance is of more recent origin than fire insurance and certain other forms of insurance in respect of damage to property that we have already looked at.

The growth in liability insurance can be dealt with under two headings: employers' and public liability.

3E1A. Employers' liability

Where an employee is injured by the fault of the employer the right arises for that injured person to claim compensation, or 'damages', from the employer. Today, this fact is accepted as sound and just, but it was not so some one hundred and fifty years ago.

During the early part of the nineteenth century the industrialisation of Britain had brought many people to the towns and cities where work was to be found in the new factories being built there.

As has often been portrayed in word and picture, these factories were dark, dismal places where men and women spent long hours in hard and exhausting work. Apart from certain enlightened employers, the drive after more and more production resulted in appalling conditions and a disregard for safety which caused many injuries.

The view, in those days, was that an industrial injury was very much a particular risk and not the responsibility of the employer. The principle applying was one known as *volenti non fit injuria* which meant that the employee had consented to run the risk of injury by being employed.

In addition to this principle the ordinary employee would have found it extremely difficult to succeed in any claim, due to lack of money, poor education and the fact that the law allowed employers to avoid any liability for injury where the injury was caused in part by the employee himself, no matter how little he may have contributed to it. Also the liability could be avoided where the injury sustained by one employee was caused by another. This latter defence was known as *common employment* of which the judge in the case of *Priestley* v. *Fowler* (1837) said, 'What, make a master liable if one of his servants injures another! If this is allowed, where shall we stop?'

3E1B. Employers' liability legislation

In 1880 the Employers' Liability Act placed certain employees in a much better legal position. Railwaymen, miners, labourers and others now found that they could sue their employers with a slightly higher chance of success, but many of the obstacles mentioned above still persisted. 1880 was also the year in which the first specialist insurer was established, the Employers' Liability Assurance Corporation.

A significant step forward took place with the passing of the Workmens' Compensation Act 1897. This provided scale benefits, such as £300 on death and half earnings during disablement up to £1 a week regardless of proving fault. The Act lasted with alterations until 1946 when the National Insurance (Industrial Injuries) Act took its place.

As yet there was no compulsion on employers to carry insurance to provide the funds out of which claims were to be paid, although talk of compulsory insurance can be traced back to 1897. Compulsory insurance eventually came with the passing of the Employers' Liability (Compulsory Insurance) Act 1969 which was effective from 1 January, 1972.

3E1C. Public liability

Little has been reported on the historical development of public liability insurance, the provision of insurance for legal liability to pay claims to those who are injured but are not employees or to those whose property is damaged by another person.

The earliest policies, towards the last quarter of the nineteenth century, related to horse drawn coaches and this later developed into motor vehicle insurance, of which more will be said later.

There are now a number of different forms of public liability insurance, all of which will be discussed in the following chapter.

3E2. Motor insurance development

The first mechanically propelled motor vehicle appeared on British roads in 1894, and by 1898 the Law Accident and Insurance Society Ltd, was offering policies to motor vehicle owners. The business was new and many of the early companies did not survive in the competition that ensued which reduced rates to uneconomic levels.

The mushrooming use and development of the motor car followed the First World War, during which the advantages of motor vehicles had been found.

By the nineteen twenties there were so many motor vehicles on the roads that legislation was almost inevitable and in 1930 the Road Traffic Act was passed.

3E2A. Compulsory insurance

The intention of the 1930 Act, *inter alia*, was to ensure that funds would be available to compensate the innocent victims of motor accidents. This was to be provided by means of insurance against legal liability to pay damages to injured persons.

The insurance requirement applied to all users of motor vehicles except where some special legal arrangment is in force. Further legislation followed in the Road Traffic Act 1960, the Motor Vehicles (Passenger Insurance) Act 1972 and the Road Traffic Act 1974 so that today insurance must be in force to cover legal liability to pay damages to any person, including others in the car, arising out of injury.

The various types of motor insurance, private car, commercial vehicle, motor cycles, motor trade and insurance for special vehicles such as cranes and excavators, form a large part of the business now transacted by many insurance companies.

3E3. Suretyship, credit and loss of profits

The forms of insurance dealt with under this heading are often referred to as pecuniary insurances as they relate to the loss of money, by one means or another, as opposed to damage to property or legal liability.

Suretyship, or fidelity guarantee, insurance caters for the risk of losing money by the fraud or dishonesty of some other person. People who held positions of responsibility often had others act as surety, or in other words guarantee to refund any money misappropriated by them in the course of their business.

Providing these sureties was a very hazardous activity, and in 1840 the Guarantee Society was formed to provide the surety by means of a policy of insurance. Five years later, in 1845, the British Guarantee Society was formed in Edinburgh and began transacting a similar form of business.

Towards the end of the nineteenth century, in 1893, another form of pecuniary insurance began to be transacted by the Excess Insurance Company. This attempted to meet the risk that a person might sell goods and the purchaser may not pay for them. This became known as credit insurance and by 1918 a specialist company was formed; it is called the Trade Indemnity Company and is still operating today. For foreign transactions the government established in 1920 the Export Credit Scheme now known as the Export Credits Guarantee Department.

Loss of profits, or business interruption, insurance is the third form of cover mentioned in the heading and such policies began to appear at the start of the twentieth century. Those policies endeavour to relieve the hardship associated with consequential loss following fire. The fire policy may cover the material damage and relieve the hardship involved in repair or rebuilding work but it does not provide any compensation for lost profit or the other financial consequences of fire.

A comparatively new form of insurance protection, within the last ten years, is the provision of cover for legal expenses. The risk being faced by a person or company is looked upon as being the uncertainty over whether or not legal expenses may be incurred and, if incurred, what they may amount to. In return for an annual premium the insured person can be freed from this uncertainty as the insurer agrees to meet legal costs subject to certain exceptions.

3F. Common features of insurance development

On looking back over the development of the different forms of insurance dealt with in this chapter a number of common features are apparent. By way of conclusion, therefore, we could list the following as being the main common features:

(a) Each class of insurance developed in response to a demand for protection. This is easily seen in the case of fire, life, liability and the other classes. The demand for protection was not always motivated by the eventual purchasers. Employers' liability and motor insurance were made compulsory by statute, thus increasing demand. The moves of Parliament in passing the appropriate legislation could, however, be looked upon as the expression of the people's desire to see protection purchased.

(b) The development of the various forms of insurance was accompanied by a measure of government supervision. We will look at this question in more detail in chapter 7 but in the meantime we should note the interest with which successive governments have viewed the development of insurance.

(c) In the main, insurance companies started off as specialist companies offering insurance in one or two types of insurance only. A feature of insurance development has been the way in which these specialist companies have expanded the forms of cover they wrote. Today there are very few specialist companies other than life and pensions companies and the majority offer many different forms of insurance. In chapter 5 we shall look at the various different types of insurance companies operating today.

(d) Today most insurance companies have gathered considerable experience in many forms of insurance. They have also collated statistics and have access to data collected by government and other bodies, which assist in arriving at reasonable premiums to charge. On looking back, however, a feature of the development of insurance was the absence of any reliable statistical information on future losses.

(e) A further feature, perhaps following on from the previous point, has been the way in which insurance companies joined together over the years to pool resources. This had many advantages, some of which were discussed in this chapter. The association of insurance companies, all offering protection against the same kind of risk, could classify the risks, pool statistics and come up with common wordings and rates.

(f) One feature which is quite striking is the success with which most insurance companies transacted their business. Bearing in mind the risky nature of their enterprise, the absence of reliable statistics and, in many cases the absence of adequate fire fighting or security services, the industry prospered. Today the vast funds, as we saw in chapter 2, represent a major source of investment for the country.

(g) A possible explanation for the relative security of insurers in these uncertain times could be the growth of reinsurance. A feature of the development of insurance was the way in which insurance companies themselves sought financial protection. This insurance bought by insurance companies is termed reinsurance and is now an essential part of the insurance market place.

(h) One final feature of the development of insurance is of more recent origin and refers to the way in which insurance companies began to combine different classes of insurance. We have seen how specialist companies began writing other forms of insurance and so became composite insurers. Similarly these composite insurance companies began combining different forms of cover in one policy. A good example of this is the way companies put fire, theft, liability and other forms of cover together in one policy for the householder and termed it the household combined or household comprehensive policy. Combined or comprehensive policies are now a common feature with many companies.

4. Classes of insurance

4A. Classifications

Over the decades and centuries as insurance has developed, the various types of cover have been grouped into several classes. These classifications have come about by practice within insurance company offices, and by the influence of legislation controlling the financial aspects of transacting insurance. The government supervision of insurance is dealt with in detail in chapter 7, but a comparison of the practical and legistic classifications is appropriate here.

4A1. Practical classifications

Insurance offices are generally split up into departments or sections, each of which will deal with types of risk which have an affiliation with each other. See figure 4/1.

Depending on the amount of business transacted some branches may split, say, the accident department into several distinct sections or departments, while on the other hand if the amount of business written is relatively small the accident and liability departments may be combined. There is also a tendency to create 'personal' depart-

Figure 4/1. Classification of insurance by department

(a)   Fire (including business interruption)
(b)   Accident (including, theft, all risks, goods-in-transit (on land), glass, money), credit and fidelity, contingency
(c)   Liability (employers', public, products and professional indemnity)
(d)   Motor
(e)   Engineering (property damage, and liabilities)
(f)   Marine & aviation
(g)   Life and pensions

ments handling all non-life business for the private individual, thus leaving the other departments to concentrate on the more intricate commercial and industrial risks.

4A2. Statutory classifications

The effect of successive British statutes and the influence of the European Economic Communicty (the EEC) on British legislation has led to the classifications shown in chapter 7. There are about 24 different classes of business, but they can, however, be grouped into 10 broad designations as shown in figure 4/2.

Figure 4/2. Designations into which classes of insurance are grouped

4B. Ordinary life assurance

We will now consider the various forms of ordinary life assurance and some special features that apply to life assurance.

4B1. Term assurance

This is the simplest and oldest form of assurance and provides for payment of the sum assured on death, provided death occurs within a specified term. Should the life assured survive to the end of the term then the cover ceases and no money is payable. Depending on the age of the assured this is a very cheap form of cover and suitable, for example, in the case of a young married man with medium to low income who wants to provide a reasonable sum for his wife in the event of his death. It can also be used for a variety of specific purposes such as business journeys.

4B2. Decreasing term assurance

This modification of term assurance is designed to cover the outstanding balance of a monthly repayment building society mortgage. As the borrower gradually repays the capital sum, so the sum assured diminishes year by year until exhausted at the end of the mortgage period. Unfortunately, since mortgage interest rates have been fluctuating in recent years, the sum assured may not be an exact fit to the outstanding loan on death. Frequently it is coupled to an endowment assurance of an amount equal to 20% or 25% of the total initial cover.

4B3. Convertible term assurance

This is similar to term assurance but a clause in the contract allows the assured to convert the policy into an endowment or whole of life contract at normal rates without medical evidence. A young person can therefore purchase low cost life cover and convert it into the more expensive types as his career progresses and he can afford more suitable contracts.

4B4. Family income benefits

In its basic form this is a type of decreasing term assurance with the benefit on death paid out by instalments every month or quarter. Frequently it is coupled to an endowment assurance like those sometimes linked to decreasing term assurances.

In each case, under the basic term, decreasing term, convertible term, or family income policy, the benefit is only paid if the life assured dies within the term of the policy. In the case of those with an endowment element the benefit will be paid on death within the policy period, or the endowment part on survival to the end of the period. Figure 4/3 illustrates the level of cover under each basic form over a number of years.

4B5. Whole life assurance

The sum assured is payable on the death of the assured whenever it occurs. Premiums are payable throughout the life of the assured or, more normally, until retiral of the assured at sixty or sixty-five. Although premiums may cease at, say, age sixty the policy is still in force and should the person die at age seventy-five the policy would provide the benefits for his representatives.

4B6. Endowment assurance

The sum assured is payable in the event of death within a specified period of years, say 15, 20, 25, or 30. However, if the life assured survives until the end of this period, until the 'maturity date', the sum assured will also be paid. For the same amount of cover, the endowment has the highest premium, because the life assurance company is guaranteeing to pay out the sum assured at a given date, or before it if the person dies. The maturity date is usually no later than the date when the life assured will reach 65. The whole life assurance mentioned earlier will be slightly cheaper than a long term endowment because the average policy will not become a claim by death until a person is in his or her seventies. The company have the premiums to invest for a longer period and can charge lower premiums. The shorter the term of an endowment policy the more expensive per £1000 it becomes since the company has fewer years in which to collect premiums.

Figure 4/3. Levels of cover under various form of term assurance

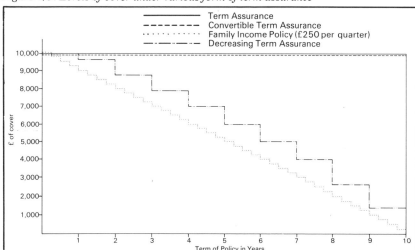

Endowment assurance is very popular with those buying houses. The assurance policy is taken out for the amount of the loan, or mortgage if a building society is involved, and written in such a way that the sum assured is payable to the lender or society. The borrower then pays the interest and the premium. At the end of the term of the loan the endowment policy matures and repays the amount borrowed, the capital sum, to the lender. In the unlooked-for event of the borrower dying prior to the end of the repayment period then he has paid up the interest to date and as there is an endowment policy in force it will mature and repay the capital sum.

This can be an expensive method of protecting a loan for house purchase and many building societies are now prepared to accept modifications involving convertible or decreasing term and endowment combination which are considerably less expensive but still provide the same security.

4B7.Assurances for children

Many people wish to make special arrangements for their children and two common schemes are the child's deferred assurance and the school fees policy.

Under a child's deferred assurance a policy is effected on the life of a parent with an 'option' date normally coinciding with the child's eighteenth or twenty-first birthday. Should the parent survive until the option date the child has the option of continuing the policy in his own name from then on, as either an endowment or whole life. The policy can be continued without further medical examination and this can be extremely important where a child has contracted an illness which would otherwise make effecting a policy difficult or extremely expensive. A lump sum can also be taken at the option date rather than continue cover. In the event of the parent dying before the option date the policy is continued, without payment of premiums, until the option date. Should the child die before the stated age the premiums can be returned to the parent or the policy continued.

Provision for school fees can be made by effecting an endowment policy, on the life of the parent, payable in instalments over the period of schooling.

4B8.More than one life

Policies may be effected on more than one life, the sum assured being payable either on the death of the first life or on the death of the last survivor. Another special type of policy, a contingent assurance, provides for payment of the sum assured on the death of one life if that takes place during the lifetime of another.

4B9.Group life assurances

Employers sometimes arrange special terms for life assurance for their employees, with the sum assured being payable in the event of death of an employee during his term of service with the employer. Membership of the scheme is open to all employees working on the inception date or the anniversary date in future years.

One policy is issued to the firm and each employee is given a certificate of membership. If an employee leaves the firm he will usually have the option of continuing the cover and converting his certificate into an individual policy at an increased premium.

4B10. Insured pension schemes

There are over nine million people in pension and life assurance schemes in Britain for which the total annual premium, paid by members and employers, is over £1,320,000,000.

These schemes provide a variety of benefits for members but the main aim is to ensure that some form of pension is available on retirement. This is a very special area both from the point of view of benefits available and method of premium payments. What we might say is that life assurance companies perform a vital role in running pension schemes. Those constructing a scheme may approach a company to (a) organize the whole scheme, receive premium contributions, invest the funds and administer the pensions, (b) manage the fund of a pension scheme, or (c) provide life assurance benefits for widows of scheme members who die before retirement.

Many employers' pension schemes are insured by means of group or master policies issued to the employer or to the trustees of the scheme. These provide retirement pensions and other benefits in respect of the employees who are eligible for the scheme, usually related to their service and salary.

A record-keeping and administration service is usually provided in association with the issue of the policy. The contract may be based on one of the types of policy used in ordinary life assurance, for example endowment assurances, or annuities as described later, or it may be specially devised for the purpose. The extent to which there is a transfer of risk varies considerably, and in some cases the main emphasis is on the provision of an investment service by the insurance company.

In association with the provision of retirement benefits, policies are usually issued insuring death in service benefits for those employees who do not reach retirement age. These may be in the form of group life assurance as described in the preceding section, or of widows' pensions

4B10A. Pensions for self-employed

Tax reliefs within statutory limits similar to those obtainable in respect of pension schemes may be obtained by the self-employed and others who are not eligible for an employer's pension scheme. Special deferred annuity policies in the prescribed form are issued to individuals who wish to take advantage of this facility.

4B11. Investment linked life assurance policies and pensions

There are various types of contracts available whereby 90–95 per cent of premiums are invested in unit trusts (an association of investors who pool their savings to form a fund which is invested by investment specialists) and the balance of the premium used to purchase term assurance.

These types of policy are closely linked to the income and profits tax regulations operating from time to time. For example, investment trusts and property bonds have been used as well, and the budget each year may change the appropriateness of the type of investment. The reader is advised to obtain prospectuses from life offices each year to ascertain the current forms of contract on offer.

4B12. Annuities

Certain of the assurances mentioned above have had the aim of ensuring an income of one form or another. An annuity is a method by which a person can receive a yearly sum, an annuity, in return for the payment to an insurance company of a sum of money. This is not life assurance as we have described it but it is dealt with by life assurance companies and is based on actuarial principles.

When a person has a reasonably large sum of money and wants to provide an income for himself after he retires or at some other time he can approach a life assurance company and purchase an annuity. The annuity may start at once, an immediate annuity, or may start at some date in the future, a deferred annuity. Regardless of when it starts it can take various forms. It may provide an annuity for the life of the person, the annuitant, or it may be payable irrespective of death for a certain period, as in the case of the annuity certain. The guaranteed annuity is similar in that it provides the annuity for a guaranteed period or until the annuitant dies. The reversionary annuity provides for payment to the annuitant, say, the wife, on the death of another named person, say, the husband. The joint and last survivor annuity is payable while two people, husband and wife, are alive and on the death of one will continue at the same or smaller rate on the life of the survivor.

4B13. Special features of life assurance

The provision of life assurance is a quite different process from the provision of non-life insurance. The main distinction is that in life assurance the event being assured is certain to happen in the case of those policies paying on death, or is scientifically calculable in the event of policies not paying a benefit on death.

4B13A. Premium payments

As we saw in chapter 3 premiums are payable by level amounts throughout the period of the policy. This means that each person pays the same amount throughout, that amount being determined by his age on effecting the policy. Premiums can be paid annually, half-yearly, quarterly or monthly and are often met by standing orders with banks whereby the policyholder instructs his bank to make the appropriate payments at the right times.

4B13B. Participation in profits

Life assurance companies value their assets and liabilities at regular intervals, some every year and others every three years. This valuation of their operation allows them to determine if any surplus exists after calculating all future liaibilities and other contingencies. Should such a surplus exist it is distributed among those policyholders who have 'with profits' or 'participating' policies. Such policies allow the policyholder to participate in any profits the company makes. It does not guarantee a bonus to each policyholder, as the company may not have a surplus, but it does mean that any available surplus will be distributed.

The policyholder pays an additional amount for the privilege of participating in profits and the bonuses are added to the sum assured and payable at the maturity date. The bonuses themselves are either simple reversionary bonuses that are computed at a rate percent on the sum assured or compound reversionary that are calculated on sum assured plus any existing bonus payments that had already been declared.

4B13C. Surrender values

When a person no longer wants his policy or for some reason cannot continue the premiums he can ask for the surrender value. He ceases payment and receives, not a proportion of the sum assured, but a proportion of the premiums. Not all policies allow a surrender value but where one is possible it will usually be less than the aggregate amount of all premiums paid. Surrender within the first few years of the existence of a policy will not normally produce any amount for the policyholder. This is due to the fact that expenses have been incurred in issuing and renewing the policy and also life assurance cover has been provided during the years it was in force. These two factors have to be paid for and therefore in the early years, in view of the level premium system, any surrender value will be low if in fact any accrues at all.

4B13D. Paid-up policies

An alternative with some policies to the surrender value is the paid-up policy. In this case the premiums cease, the policy continues, but on maturity a smaller sum than would originally have been paid will be due to the policyholder. Depending on the policy and the company concerned these paid-up policies may or may not continue to participate in profits.

4B13E. Tax relief

Until the Budget of 1984 certain policyholders were entitled to tax relief on life assurance premiums. Relief was granted provided:
- (a) the policy qualified for tax relief. The rules for qualification were fairly complex but the majority of policies were eligible;
- (b) the policy was on the life of the income tax payer or that of his or her spouse:
- (c) the premiums were paid by the income tax payer or his/her spouse.

Prior to 6 April 1979 a person paid the full, gross premium and subsequently received the appropriate tax relief in the form of an allowance included in his tax coding. Following the Finance Act 1976 the system changed from 6 April 1979 and each person paid the net premium, after tax relief, to the insurance company and the company claimed the balance, representing the tax relief, from the Inland Revenue. The rate of relief was 15 per cent of gross premiums payable subject to premiums not exceeding £1500 or one-sixth of income, whichever is the higher. Those who were not taxpayers benefited from the new system as everyone, regardless of whether they paid income tax or not, enjoyed the benefit of the relief. Now no tax relief is given on life assurance premiums.

4B13F. Investments

We have already identified the life assurance industry as being of considerable size. This was evidenced by the number of policies in force and the value of premiums paid each year. These vast amounts of money are held by companies to meet future liabilities and are termed life assurance funds. The total value of such funds for ordinary life assurance in 1982 was some £67,500m.

These funds do not lie dormant waiting for claims to come in; they are invested to provide income for the companies and so assist policyholders and shareholders. Not only do these two groups benefit, but the country as a whole benefits as the funds are invested in many forms that encourage expansion of industry and promote employment. A look around any town or city will reveal how many new building projects are sponsored by life assurance companies.

These companies are the 'institutional investors' often referred to on radio, television and in the newspapers.

4C. Industrial life assurance

There are many more industrial life assurance policies in force than ordinary life policies, but they are for smaller amounts. The 71.9 million policies in force at the end of 1982 produced yearly premiums of £1,070m. Therefore while there were nearly three times as many industrial policies as there were ordinary policies they produced about one third of the premiums paid under ordinary life assurance policies.

Endowment and whole life assurances are the most popular forms of contract in the industrial assurance sector, normally with low sums assured. It is also common to see recurring endowments which provide whole life cover and the payment of small amounts at regular intervals, say every five years.

The function of industrial life assurance, as distinct from that of ordinary life assurance, is to bring life assurance to those who by reason of circumstances would not normally be interested in carrying assurance cover. They are of the lower income class, and it has been recognised that the only way in which life policies once effected by such assured can be expected to be maintained is by the collection of premiums at the homes of the policyholders. It is also acknowledged that such policyholders will not exercise the self-discipline necessary if sums of money have to be saved to meet yearly, half-yearly or even quarterly premiums. Premium payments, therefore, under industrial assurance contracts are made at more frequent intervals than under ordinary life assurance contracts – each premium payment is smaller and a call on the policyholder is made for it.

4D. Accident and health
4D1. Personal accident insurance

The intention of the basic policy is to provide compensation in the event of an accident causing death or injury. What are termed capital sums are paid in the event of death or certain specified injuries, such as the loss of limbs or sight as may be defined in the policy.

The policy is usually extended to include a weekly benefit up to 104 weeks or compensation if the insured is temporarily totally disabled due to an accident and a reduced weekly benefit if he is temporarily only partially disabled from carrying out his normal duties.

In the event of permanent total disablement (other than loss of eyes or limbs) an annuity is paid.

In addition to the purchase of personal accident insurance by individuals it is also possible for companies to arrange cover on behalf of their employees and many organisations arrange 'group schemes' to this end.

4D2. Sickness insurance

Personal accident cover can be extended to provide a weekly benefit up to 104 weeks if the insured is temporarily totally disabled from engaging in his usual occupation due to sickness.

Personal accident and sickness policies are renewable annually and if a claim has occurred which could be of a recurring nature, the cover may be restricted at renewal or in severe cases renewal not offered.

4D3. Permanent health insurance

This type of cover has been devised to overcome the limitation of 104 weeks' maximum benefit under the personal accident and sickness policies and provide benefits for those who are disabled for longer periods, or who, because of accident or illness, have to change to a lower paid occupation.

It is usual to arrange cover to exclude the first month, six months or twelve months of disablement with appropriate discounts in the premium rates, since many people will receive a substantial part of their salaries for a certain period when off work. Cover cannot continue beyond age 65 and in order to save premium some people elect for cover to cease at age 55 or 60. The maximum benefit payable is usually 66 per cent or 75 per cent of earnings less other disability benefits payable.

4E. Motor insurance
4E1. Scope of motor insurance

The minimum requirement by law is to provide insurance in respect of legal liability to pay damages arising out of injury caused to any person. A policy for this risk only is available and is termed an 'Act only' policy. These are not at all common and usually reserved for a situation where the risk is exceptionally high. A 'third party only' policy would satisfy the minimum legal requirements and in addition would include cover for legal liability where damage was caused to some other person's property. An addition to the form of cover is where damage to the car itself from fire or theft is included, a 'third party, fire and theft policy'.

The most common form of cover is the 'comprehensive policy' which adds accidental loss of or damage to the vehicle to the third party, fire and theft cover. Figure 4/4 shows the forms of motor insurance cover.

4E2. Classes of motor insurance
4E2A. Private car insurance

This class relates to private cars used for social and domestic purposes and/or business purposes. Comprehensive policies issued to individuals also include personal accident benefits for insured and spouse, medical expenses and loss of or damage to rugs, clothing and personal effects.

Figure 4/4. Forms of motor insurance cover

Road Traffic Act only	Third party only	Third Party, Fire and Theft	Comprehensive
Legal liability for death or injury to any person by use of a motor vehicle	R.T.A. cover plus Legal liability for damage to other persons' property	Third party cover plus Fire and/or theft loss or damage to the vehicle	Third party, Fire and theft cover plus Other accidental loss of or damage to the vehicle

4E2B. Commercial vehicle policies

All vehicles used for commercial purposes, lorries, taxis, vans, hire cars, milk floats, police cars etc. are not insured under private car policies but under special contracts known as commercial vehicle policies.

4E2C. Motor cycles

This is a growing sector of motor insurance business and may well continue to be so if petrol becomes more and more scarce. The type of policy depends upon the machine, whether it is a moped or a high powered motor cycle and on the age and experience of the cyclist. The cover is comparatively inexpensive relative to motor car insurance.

4E2D. Motor trade

Special policies are offered to garages and other people within the motor trade to ensure that their liability is covered while using vehicles on the road. Damage to vehicles in garages and showrooms can also be included under such policies.

4E2E. Special types

The present classification of insurance business refers to 'land vehicles other than railway rolling stock' and many such vehicles fall under a category known to insurers as 'special types'. These will include forklift trucks, mobile cranes, bulldozers and excavators. Such vehicles may travel on roads as well as building sites and other private ground. Where special type vehicles are not used on roads, they are transported from site to site and it is more appropriate to insure the liability under a public liability policy, as the vehicle is really being used as a 'tool of trade' rather than a motor vehicle.

4F. Marine and transport insurance
4F1. Marine insurance
4F1A. Forms of policy

Marine policies relate to three areas of risk, the hull, cargo and freight. The risks against which these items are normally insured are collectively termed, 'perils of the sea' and include fire, theft, collision and a wide range of other perils. While hull and cargo are self-explanatory the word freight may not be. Freight is the sum paid for transporting goods or for the hire of a ship. When goods are lost by marine perils then freight, or part of it, is lost, hence the need for cover.

(a) *Time policy*. This is for a fixed period usually not exceeding 12 months.
(b) *Voyage policy*. Operative for the period of the voyage. For cargo the cover is from warehouse to warehouse.
(c) *Mixed policy*. Covers the subject matter for the voyage and a period of time thereafter e.g., while in port.
(d) *Building risk policy*. Covers the construction of marine vessels.
(e) *Floating policy*. This provides the policy holder with a large reserve of cover for cargo. A large initial sum is granted and each time shipments are sent the insured declares this and the value of the shipment is deducted from the outstanding sum insured.
(f) *Small craft*. The increasing leisure use of small boats brought about the introduction of a policy aimed at this form of craft. It is comprehensive in style, covering a wide range of perils including liability insurance.

4F1B. Policy administration

Apart from small craft policies which are written and issued by many companies, all marine policies are written on the standard MAR form. This is a blank policy form and is added to by various clauses both for hull and cargo insurances.

4F1C. Marine cargo

Cargo is usually insured on a warehouse (of departure) to warehouse (of arrival) basis and frequently covering all risks.

4F1D. Marine liabilities

The custom has been to provide insurance for three-quarters of the shipowner's liability for collisions at sea under the marine policy. The remaining quarter and all other forms of liability are catered for by associations set up for the purpose by shipowners and known as Protecting and Indemnity Clubs (P and I clubs).

4G. Aviation insurance

The use of aircraft as a means of transport is increasing each year and because of the specialist and technical nature of the risks associated with it, and the high potential cost of accidents, all aviation risks, from component parts to complete jumbo jets, are insured in the aviation insurance market.

4G1. Forms of policy

Most policies are issued on an 'all risks' basis subject to certain restrictions. The buyers of these policies are the large commercial airlines, the corporate or business aircraft owners, private owners and flying clubs. Usually a comprehensive policy is issued covering the aircraft itself (the hull), the liabilities to passengers and the liabilities to others.

4G2. Aviation liabilities

Liability for accidents to passengers is governed by a maze of international agreements and national laws around the world. The main ones are the Warsaw Convention 1929 which made signatories liable to passengers without negligence but subject to certain maxima amounts and the Hague Protocol 1955 which raised some of these limits. The national laws may place higher limits on domestic flights. It is interesting to note that in *Goldman* v. *Thai Airlines International* (1981) it was held that the limits did not apply when the aircrew were 'reckless' in flying the aircraft. The two international agreements also place limits on liability for goods carried by air.

Other groups of persons requiring aviation liability cover are aircraft and aircraft component manufacturers, and airport authorities.

4G3. Insurance of air cargo

Unless of special risk or value, cargo is usually insured 'all risks' in the marine or general markets rather than the aviation market.

4H. Fire and other property damage insurance
4H1. Fire insurance
4H1A. Standard fire policy

A standard fire policy is used for almost all business insurances, with Lloyd's of London also issuing a standard fire policy that is slightly different in its wording.

The basic intention of the fire policy is to provide compensation to the insured person in the event of there being damage to the property insured.

4H1B. Insured perils

It is not possible, in the commercial world, to issue a policy that will provide compensation regardless of how the damage occurs. The insurance company, the insurers, have to know the perils they are insuring.

The standard fire policy covers damage to property caused by fire, lightning or explosion, where this explosion is brought about by gas or boilers not used for any industrial purpose.

This is limited in its scope as property can be damaged in other ways, and to meet this need a number of extra perils, known as special perils, can be added on to the basic policy. These perils are:

— storm tempest or flood	— riot, civil commotion
— burst pipes	— malicious damage
— earthquake	— explosion
— aircraft	— impact

It is important to remember that these additional perils must result in damage to the property, and it is as well to precede each by saying, 'damage to the property caused by . . .'

4H1C. The property insured

In most commercial policies the insured will require cover for buildings, machinery and plant, and stock. These are the three main headings under which property is insured and in some cases a list of such items can run to many pages, depending upon the size of the insured company.

In addition to these areas it may be necessary to arrange cover for property while it is still being built, i.e. buildings in course of erection, but this form of cover is gradually giving way to a policy known as 'contractors' all risks' which will be referred to later.

4H2. Theft insurance

Theft policies have the same aim as the standard fire policy in that they intend to provide compensation to the insured in the event of loss of the property insured.

The property to be insured, for a commercial venture, will be the same as under the fire policy except of course the buildings. The theft policy will, in addition, show a more detailed definition of the stock. The reason for this is that fire is indiscriminate and a thief is not, so the insurers charge more for stock which is attractive to thieves.

The law relating to theft was brought up to date by the Theft Act 1968. This had an immediate impact on insurance companies as it defined the term 'theft'. The legal definition was wider than that which the companies were prepared to offer, especially for business premises, as the definition did not mention any need for there to be force and violence in committing a theft. This meant that shoplifting, for example, was 'theft' and this kind of risk had traditionally been uninsurable. To remedy the problem insurance companies included in their policies a phrase to the effect that theft, within the meaning of the policy, was to include force and violence either in breaking in to or out of the premises of the insured.

4H3. All risks insurance

Uncertainty of loss is not restricted to events brought about by fire or theft, nor is it limited to events occurring on or about the insured's premises. This realization led, as we noted earlier, to the development of a wider form of cover known as all risks. The term 'all risks' is unfortunate in the sense that it does not provide cover against all risks, as there are a number of exceptions, but it is an improvement on the scope of cover available.

4H3A. Personal effects

All risks policies are very popular with individuals who seek a wider protection than that afforded by the policies available to cover household effects.

The all risks policy can be taken out on particularly expensive items such as jewellery, cameras and fur coats, and can also be arranged on unspecified goods for a lump sum. The twin objectives of such policies are to provide cover for the whole range of accidental loss or damage and to do so wherever the goods themselves happen to be at the time of loss.

4H3B. Business all risks

The use of all risks policies in the commercial sector is becoming more popular as expensive and sophisticated pieces of machinery are introduced to the factory and the office.

The advent of the micro-processor and the silicon chip mean that comparatively small machines, often desk top equipment, are replacing larger and bulkier apparatus. It would be quite easy for a small desk top computer to be accidentally dropped or otherwise damaged. The small bulk conceals a high value and the owner may well consider an all risks policy to be worthwhile if it assists in removing some of the uncertainty.

4H3C. Goods-in-transit

This form of cover provides compensation to the owner of goods if the goods are damaged or lost while in transit. Different policies can be taken out depending upon whether the goods are carried by the owners' own vehicles or by a firm of carriers. In the same way the carrier can effect a policy as he is often responsible for the goods while they are in his custody.

We depend to a great extent on the carriage of goods by road and this form of cover is an important aspect of industrial activity.

Forms of goods-in-transit insurance are also available for those who send their goods by rail or by post. The compensation provided by British Rail or the Post Office is often far less than the value of the goods being carried and in such cases it is a wise precaution to have arranged adequate insurance.

We have dealt with goods-in-transit insurance here under the heading of 'damage to property' although according to the latest classification of insurance business by statute it should be handled along with motor, marine or aviation insurances.

4H3D. Contractors' all risks

This is one of the newer forms of insurance that has been developed to meet the changing needs of industry. When new buildings or civil engineering projects such as motorways or bridges are being constructed a great deal of money is invested before the work is finished. The risk is that the particular building or bridge may sustain severe damage and this would prolong the construction time and delay the eventual completion date. The risk is all the more acute as the completion date draws near, and there are many examples of buildings and other projects sustaining severe damage, and even total destruction, only days before they were to be handed over to the new owners.

Should damage occur then the contractor would have to start again, or at best repair the damage. This costs money and cannot be added on to the eventual charge the contractor will make to the owner for having carried out the building. As a result the need arose for some form of financial protection and this came with the development of contractors' all risks insurance. The intention of the policy is to provide compensation to the contractor in the event of there being damage to the construction works from a wide range of perils.

4H3E.Money insurance The loss of money represents the final form of all risks cover we will look at. The policy provides compensation to the insured in the event of money being stolen either from his business premises, his own home or while it is being carried to or from the bank. Even for a person having a medium sized business this is an extremely important form of cover as large sums of money are drawn from banks to meet wages and one only needs to look at the newspapers week by week to note the regularity with which hold-ups occur.

One important addition to this cover is often the provision of some compensation to employees who may be injured or have clothing damaged during a robbery.

4H4.Glass Cover is also available against accidental breakage of plate glass in windows and doors. In the case of shops this is often extended to include damage done to shop window contents.

4H5.Engineering As we saw earlier, the provision of engineering cover had its beginnings with boiler explosions. This still forms a major part of the work done by engineering insurers but the increasing sophistication of industry has resulted in them moving on to cover other forms of engineering plant, particularly lifts, cranes, electrical equipment, engines and, more recently, computers.

The cover is intended to provide compensation to the insured in the event of the plant insured being damaged by some extraneous cause or its own breakdown.

Engineering insurers still continue to provide an inspection service on a wide range of engineering plant and this is a service much sought after by industry not only because many forms of inspection are compulsory by law but because engineering insurers have built up a considerable expertise in this area.

Engineering cover can be summarised thus:
(a) damage to or breakdown of specific items of plant and machinery;
(b) an inspection service of those items;
(c) cost of repair of own surrounding property due to (a);
(d) legal liability for injury caused by (a);
(e) legal liability for damage to property of others caused by (a).

4I.Liability insurances We have already dealt with the liability insurance arising under the specialist branches of motor, marine and aviation, and engineering insurances. It remains to look at brief details of what is sometimes termed 'general liability' and which comprises employers' liability, public liability, products liability insurances and professional indemnity insurances.

4I1.Employers' liability insurance When an employer is held legally liable to pay damages to an injured employee or the representatives of someone fatally injured, he can claim against his employers' liability policy which will provide him with exactly the same amount he himself has had to pay out. In addition the policy will also pay certain expenses by way of lawyer's fees or doctor's charges where an injured man has been medically examined. The intention is to ensure that the employer does not suffer financially but is compensated for any money he may have to pay in respect of a claim. The policy is restricted to damages payable in respect of injury and does not apply where property of an employee is damaged.

Insurance is compulsory for all but a few employers and this has resulted in employers' liability insurance forming a large part of the insurance transacted in Britain. With each policy an annual certificate is issued which must be displayed at every place of business as evidence of the fact that the employer has complied with the law and effected a policy.

4I2.Public liability insurance Members of the public may suffer injury or damage to their property due to the activities of someone else, and the public liability insurances have been designed to provide compensation for those who may have to pay damages and legal costs for such injuries or for the damage to property. Particular types of policy are available for each type of risk.

4I2A.Business risks policy Every business organisation is exposed to the risk of incurring legal liability due to its operations. The public may be in contact with the firm in its offices or the firm may be on the premises of others in the street or on various sites. The policy will indemnify the insured for liabilities thus incurred.

4I2B.Products liability insurance

An exception on most business public liability policies is one relating to liability arising out of goods sold. This is a very onerous liability and one that insurers would prefer to deal with separately. If a person is injured by any product he purchases, foodstuffs for example, and he can show that the seller, or in some cases the manufacturer, was to blame he could succeed in a claim for damages.

We have already seen that liability arising out of products which are likely to find their way into the construction of aircraft are dealt with by aviation insurance departments.

4I2C.Professional liability

Another exception on the basic public liability policy is one relating to liability arising out of professional negligence. This can arise where lawyers, accountants, doctors, insurance brokers and a whole range of professional men do or say things that result in others suffering in some sense. A lawyer may give advice carelessly that results in the person who was relying on the advice losing money. That person would be able to sue the lawyer for an amount equal to what he had lost. The lawyer can effect professional liability insurance, often known as professional indemnity insurance, to meet the cost of any award against him.

4I2D.Personal public liability

Each individual owes a duty to his neighbour not to cause them injury or damage their property. Liability may arise out of the ownership of a house, a pet, out of sporting activities or just in the simple act of crossing the road without looking. The case of *Clark* v. *Shepstone* (1968) emphasizes the need for personal public liability cover. Mrs. Shepstone stepped from the pavement without looking and caused a motor cyclist to swerve. The bike crashed and the pillion passenger, Mr. Clark, suffered severe injury. He sued Mrs. Shepstone and eventually accepted £28,500. In the absence of a personal public liability policy Mrs. Shepstone would have been in serious financial difficulties.

4J.Credit and suretyship insurances
4J1.Credit insurance

Traders can sustain heavy losses by reason of insolvency or protracted default on the part of buyers of their goods, and credit insurance can afford the requisite protection. In overseas trade it may be impossible for customers to pay for goods because of the outbreak of war or government restrictions on remittances, and this so-called 'political risk' can be covered with the ordinary insolvency risk with the Export Credits Guarantee Department. No private insurer could bear so heavy a risk; it is one essentially for a government department.

4J2.Suretyship or fidelity guarantee insurances

The object of this class of business is to provide insurance against loss by reason of the dishonesty of persons holding positions of trust, while for some guarantees the protection goes beyond dishonesty to cover loss caused by mistake, as, for instance, where a liquidator maladministers the affairs of a company being wound up by reason of a mistake in law.

The main divisions are noted below.

4J2A.Commercial guarantees

These will be effected by employers in respect of persons who have some post within the company where they may be in a position to perpetrate some form of fraud.

4J2B.Local government bonds

These are the local government equivalent of the commercial guarantees described above.

4J2C.Court bonds

From time to time it is necessary for the courts to entrust the property or affairs of an individual to someone else, but before doing so they will require that 'administrator' to supply a bond or financial guarantee which can be utilised to make good losses due to malpractice. Property which requires to be looked after pending the result of litigation and the administration of the affairs of minors or those not mentally capable of administering their own affairs are examples of situations when bonds would be required.

4J2D.Government bonds

Another common example is the Customs and Excise Bond which guarantees that if dutiable goods, intended for export and on which no duty is payable, find their way into the home market or are stolen, the duty will be paid by the surety should the owner or manufacturer fail to pay.

4K.General (or other) insurances
4K1.Insurance of rent

When a building has been damaged, let us say quite badly damaged so that it cannot be used until repairs are carried out, the person occupying the building may still be obliged contractually to pay rent to the owner. In a similar case the owner may lose rent where the tenant has been relieved of the obligation to pay it.

4K2.Interruption insurance

This form of insurance was originally called time loss, then loss of profits, or consequential loss, and towards the latter part of the 1970s 'interruption insurance'. This last title is appropriate because the policies available deal with the loss of profits of a business or the additional expenditure necessary after some physical property has been damaged.

The fire, all risks or engineering policies already mentioned earlier in this chapter will deal with the value of the property damaged or destroyed but not with the losses which reduced sales have brought about during the repair period and thereafter until full sales are restored. These losses come about because:

(a) certain overhead costs will remain at their full level even though sales are reduced;

(b) net profit will be reduced;

(c) there may be certain increases in costs incurred to keep the business going in a temporary manner.

The most common interruption policies are those which cover losses flowing from:

(a) fire and special perils;

(b) engineering breakdown risks;

(c) computer damage and breakdown risks.

4K3. Legal expenses insurance

Cover is available to private individuals and organisations both of whom now face an ever-increasing possibility of legal action. One growing area of cover is among trade unions and professional bodies. Many of such organisations offer a legal service as one of the benefits of membership but with escalating costs it is very difficult for them to budget. To ease the problem they can purchase legal expenses insurance and pay a fixed premium each year.

4K4. Miscellaneous insurances

Whenever there is a demand for a particular cover and the criteria for insurable risks (see chapter 2) have been met, the industry will usually provide the covers necessary.

Examples of such policies include livestock, weather (rain and sunshine deficiency), twins or multiple births, loss of licence, kidnap and ransom, strikes, and aquaculture (fish farms).

4L. Combined and comprehensive policies

Many of the forms of cover already dealt with are required by the same individual or business. A householder who owns and occupies his own house will require fire, special perils, loss of rent, additional living costs if the house is damaged, theft, glass, money and liability insurances. The industrial purchaser may require the same with the possible addition of goods-in-transit, engineering, fidelity, credit and loss of profits insurances.

4L1. Combined insurances

The advantages of combining various forms of insurance into one policy form can be said to be:

(a) less costly from the administrative point of view;

(b) only one premium and one renewal date to bother about;

(c) less chance of overlooking one form of cover;

(d) easier to market as one product rather than several independent policies.

These combined policies, sometimes known as 'traders' combined' or 'shopkeepers' combined', are very suitable for a large number of business insureds although the larger the insured becomes the greater the need to arrange insurances specially for him.

Another example is the holiday and travel insurance policy where all risks cover is combined with personal accident, medical expenses, loss of deposits and delay covers on one policy.

4L2. Comprehensive insurances

A step on from issuing combined policies, which is only the combination of separate policies within the one folder, is the comprehensive policy. This form of cover represents a widening in the scope of cover. This is evidenced by the household comprehensive policy which, in addition to covering the basic perils mentioned above, also includes cover against damage caused by collapse of television aerials, leakage of central heating oil and the breakage of underground water pipes, sanitary fittings and many more risks. This widening of scope of the perils insured has been accompanied by alterations in the basic method of providing cover so that today it is possible to arrange a household comprehensive policy which provides cover against damage caused by almost any event with the amount being paid representing what it will actually cost to replace the damaged property.

This widening in cover has not been without its problems and many insurers have experienced substantial losses on their household insurance business, as a result of which substantial increases in premiums have been introduced.

Comprehensive policies are also available for offices and shops where cover is provided as a package. This is an efficient and relatively inexpensive way to provide cover for small offices and shops.

4M.Space risks   One modern development is the provision of insurance to those who are involved with satellites. Ever since the first Sputnik–1 was launched in October 1957 it was inevitable that the commercial use of space satellites would eventually follow. These satellites are now used for a wide range of telecommunications purposes. A number of risks can now be covered in the Marine market, the main ones being material damage, during testing or launch as well as while in orbit, and loss of revenue.

5. The market place

5A.General structure of the market place

When one talks about a market place, a vision of a Saturday market in a country town, or a cattle market, or some similar meeting place, springs to mind. Most of us have seen pictures in books, or in the media, of markets being held for the sale of grain, tobacco leaf, or stocks and shares.

In the market for insurance, however, there is no single place in the country or in a town where the buyers, sellers and middlemen meet to transact insurance. There is one exception to this general statement and that is the transaction of insurance business at Lloyd's which will be discussed in full a little later. Suffice it to say at the moment that the organisation of the Lloyd's market is unique in the world, although a Lloyd's type market has been set up in New York and in Florida in recent times.

5A1.Insurance as a service industry

Like any other market, the insurance market comprises sellers – the insurance companies and Lloyd's underwriting members, buyers – the general public, industry and commerce, and middlemen – the insurance brokers and agents. In other markets the buyers, sellers and perhaps the middlemen can come together to examine the merchandise which is to be the subject of the sale, but with insurance it is not possible to bring the house, factory or ship etc. to a market place, and in any event what is being insured is intangible in that it is someone's financial interest in the house, factory, ship or potential lawsuit which is at risk.

Therefore, although the buying and selling of insurance takes place every hour of every working day, contracts are arranged as and when required, at a place convenient to the individual parties concerned. As was seen in chapter 2 when discussing the functions of insurance, the insurance market is providing a financial service. It is a service industry in that it is supportive to industry producing goods.

The structure of the market is shown in figure 5/1.

Figure 5/1. The insurance market

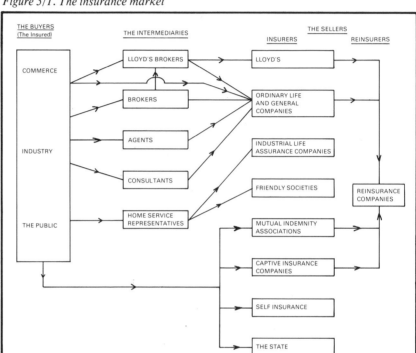

5B. The buyers

Those people who have no great knowledge of insurance and are just embarking upon their careers, probably the majority of the readers of this book, will most likely think of insurance in terms of personal insurance. They will recall the fact that they, or their parents, purchase private car insurance, household insurance, life assurance and that will be the extent of their knowledge of insurance buying. There is of course no reason why they should have any broader knowledge; domestic or personal insurances do indeed form a large part of the buying market. In 1981 the Government published a Family Expenditure Survey which revealed that the average annual expenditure of households on all forms of insurance was £242.60. Over three-quarters of all households in Britain had some expenditure on life assurance, the same number had some expenditure on household contents insurance and nearly 60% had some expenditure on motor insurance. These statistics certainly explain why most non-insurance people limit their thinking on insurance to these personal insurances.

However it is not personal insurances which occupy the bulk of the time in the insurance market, nor will the CII student spend most of his or her time studying those areas. For most insurance companies it is commercial and industrial insurance which take up the time. When you consider that one single insured, one single company, could be spending millions of pounds per year on insurance premiums you begin to get the market in perspective.

5C. The intermediaries (or middlemen)

It is possible, as can be seen from figure 5/1, to buy insurance direct. Many private individuals choose to do this. They decide what their insurance needs are, they may approach a number of insurance companies to obtain premium figures and then they decide with which company to insure.

The commercial buyer of insurance is in a slightly different position. He may be faced with half a dozen factory complexes spread throughout Britain, each one presenting many and varied forms of risk. He is in need of some expertise to enable him to assess the risks he has and to match his needs to the best seller of insurance in the market place. The majority of business is in fact handled by an intermediary of one form or another.

In legal terms an 'intermediary' is an agent i.e., one who is authorized by a party, called 'the principal', to bring that principal into a contractual relationship with another, 'a third party'. If the agent does not have prior authority to act in this way but purports to do so, and the principal later ratifies or confirms the agent's actions, then a contractual relationship will exist. (Agents can be appointed for other purposes but these are beyond the scope of the present discussions, e.g., employees can be agents of their employers.)

5C1. The insurance broker

A broker is an individual or firm whose full-time occupation is the placing of insurance with insurance companies. There are two categories of brokers:

(a) Lloyd's brokers: they are the only persons permitted to place business at Lloyd's (see later). They also place business in the company market;

(b) other brokers (just termed 'brokers').

Both categories are full-time professionals who must be registered (see chapter 7). They normally act as agents for the insured (Lloyd's brokers always so), and are remunerated by a higher rate of commission than agents. By calling themselves 'brokers' they are holding themselves out to be experts in the field of insurance and have a higher duty of care to their principals than agents.

They will generally have authority to issue cover for certain classes of insurance e.g., motor, and in some cases may issue simple policies, e.g., travel and perhaps household.

The insured can obtain independent advice on a wide range of insurance matters from a broker without direct cost to himself. For example, the broker will advise on insurance needs, best type of cover and its restrictions, best market, claims procedure, obligations placed on the insured by policy conditions, and he will up-date the information as time goes by to take account of market changes.

From the insurers' point of view, negotiations with brokers are easier and speedier as only the intricate points or special requirements require detailed discussion, thus saving time and money on routine matters.

5C1A. Lloyd's broker

The Lloyd's broker carries out the same functions as 'a broker' but if one wishes to insure at Lloyd's the business must be placed there by a Lloyd's broker.

The Committee of Lloyd's, in addition to approving the appointment of members, also appoints brokers to act as Lloyd's brokers. They require to satisfy the Committee as to their expertise, integrity and financial standing. After being appointed, they can display the words 'and at Lloyd's' on their letter heading and name plates.

The Lloyd's broker represents the insured in the transactions with the underwriter.

Although only approved brokers can enter 'The Room' and place business, the Lloyd's brokers are otherwise the same as other insurance brokers in their dealings with insurance companies.

5C2. Agents

As was mentioned above, an agent in law is one who acts for another, but in insurance the term is usually reserved for the individual or firm whose main occupation is in another field. For example, estate agents, solicitors, accountants, garage proprietors and building societies could be appointed as agents since their clients may require insurance cover and these intermediaries would arrange it.

5C3. Insurance consultants

Another category of intermediary is the insurance consultant, who may act in a similar manner to an insurance broker. If he does not call himself 'an insurance broker' he does not require to register under the Insurance Brokers' (Registration) Act 1977.

5C4. Home service insurance representative

The industrial life assurance offices and friendly societies employ representatives to call at the homes of their policyholders to collect the weekly premiums and hopefully to sell further policies. They are not intermediaries in the same way as the others. In this case the representative is employed by the assurance company but nevertheless he or she performs the function of an intermediary.

5D. The sellers or suppliers of insurance

Figure 5/1 shows nine different forms of insurance supplier; this will have surprised those who thought insurance was a simple matter of going into the High Street branch of a big insurance company and buying a policy.

We shall now look at each of these sellers in turn.

5D1. Lloyd's

Lloyd's is quite unlike any of the other sellers of insurance. At the moment we will consider the nature of Lloyd's as part of the overall insurance market and later (in 5E) we will look at the way business is actually transacted there.

In chapter 3 we charted the brief history of Lloyd's from its beginnings in Edward Lloyd's Coffee Shop. As the volume of business increased we saw that larger premises were found and a Committee was formed. In 1871 the Lloyd's Act created the

Corporation of Lloyd's. The Corporation did not transact insurance, this was still the province of individual underwriting members, but it did provide premises, services and assistance. It also, through the Council of Lloyd's, laid down the regulations and requirements which had to be met by anyone wishing to become a member.

5D1A. Lloyd's Act 1982

The latest piece of legislation relating to Lloyd's was enacted in July 1982. It was the result of an enquiry under the chairmanship of Sir Henry Fisher, into the constitution of and self-regulation at Lloyd's.

The Act created a new Council of Lloyd's. The Council has overall responsibility and control of affairs at Lloyd's, including rule-making and discipline. The Council has 28 members, 16 of which are actively and fully engaged in the business of insurance at Lloyd's. Eight other members are elected from among all those underwriting members who are not actively involved in the transaction of insurance and four persons are appointed by the Council and confirmed by the Governor of the Bank of England.

The Committee of Lloyd's comprises the 16 working members of the Council and is concerned more with the day-to-day running of affairs at Lloyd's rather than any long term planning or policy formulation.

5D1B. Membership of Lloyd's

There are over 23,000 members of Lloyd's grouped into approximately 400 Syndicates. These syndicates can be made up of only a few members or in some cases more than a thousand. Each syndicate appoints an underwriting agent to manage its affairs and this underwriting agent appoints professional underwriters on behalf of the syndicate. Later we will see just how this underwriter accepts business on behalf of his syndicate. In the meantime we should note that the *names,* the underwriting members, are not insurance professionals. They come from many walks of life including the professions, the world of entertainment, the aristocracy etc. Each underwriting member is, however, fully and personally liable for all the business written on behalf of his syndicate by the underwriter whom it employs.

In view of this *unlimited* liability it is essential that strict regulations apply to any person wishing to become an underwriting member. To become a Lloyd's underwriting member a person must:

1) be recommended by other members;
2) transact business with unlimited personal liability;
3) satisfy the Council of Lloyd's of his financial integrity;
4) furnish security in an approved form to be held in trust by the Corporation of Lloyd's; the amount varies according to the wealth of the member and the volume of business to be transacted. A member with assets of £100,000 and who produces security amounting to £50,000 could transact business involving premiums of up to £200,000 a year;
5) pay all premiums into Premium Trust Funds under deeds of trust approved by the Department of Trade and the Council of Lloyd's from which only claims, expenses and profit may be paid;
6) subject underwriting accounts annually to an independent audit which requires underwriting assets to be sufficient to meet his liabilities for all classes of business;
7) contribute by means of a levy on premium income to a Central Fund intended to meet underwriting liabilities of any member in the unlikely event of his security and personal assets being insufficient to meet his underwriting commitments. This Central Fund is not intended to protect the underwriter, who is still personally liable to the full extent of his private wealth; it is intended to protect the insured person. The Fund stands at over £100m.

5D2. Insurance companies
5D2A. Proprietary companies

The majority of insurance companies come under this heading and are limited liability companies with shareholders as proprietors.

Historically they have been created by Royal Charter, as in the case of the The Royal Exchange Assurance; by Act of Parliament, as in the case of The Scottish Union and National (now part of the Norwich Union Group); and by Deed of Settlement (a form of partnership), but generally these companies have been reformed by registration under the Companies Acts.

The majority of insurance companies have been created by registration under the Companies Acts and it is almost certain that all new companies in the future will be created in this manner.

Proprietary companies have an authorised and issued share capital to which the original shareholders subscribed, and it is to the shareholders that any profits belong after provision for expenses, reserves and, in the case of life business, with profit policyholders' bonuses. The shareholders' liability is limited to the nominal value of their shares (hence the term limited liability), but the company is liable for its debts and if the solvency margin cannot be met (see chapter 7) the company will go into liquidation. The public can deal direct with these companies but often an intermediary is involved. In most classes of business there is keen competition among proprietary companies and also between proprietary companies and other sectors of the market.

5D2B. Mutual companies

Mutual companies have been formed by Deed of Settlement or registration under the Companies Acts. They are owned by the policyholders who share any profits made. The shareholder in the proprietary company receives his share of the profit by way of dividends, but in the mutual company the policyholder owner may enjoy lower premiums or higher life assurance bonuses than would otherwise be the case.

Originally, the policyholders could be called upon to make further contributions to the fund if the original premiums were inadequate to meet the claims and expenses. Nowadays most mutual insurers are limited by guarantee with the policyholders' maximum liability limited to their premiums or, at the most, an additional 50p. or £1.

It is no longer possible to tell from the name of a company whether it is proprietary or mutual. Many companies which were originally formed as mutual organisations have now registered under the Companies Acts as proprietary companies although they have retained the word mutual in their title. Others, registered as companies limited by guarantee and without the word mutual in their title, are, in fact, owned by the policyholders.

The members or policyholders of mutual companies sometimes receive substantial benefits by way of lower premiums or higher bonuses, but this is by no means certain. Many of the large proprietary companies can compete successfully in terms of premiums or benefits with the mutuals and still pay dividends to their shareholders. The large volume of business transacted by some proprietary groups allows substantial savings to be made in administrative costs per policy and the larger investment income generated from larger reserves allow them to pass on some of these benefits to policyholders.

5D3. Classification of insurance companies

In this chapter, so far, we have classified companies according to their form of ownership, but sometimes companies can be classified in other ways:

(a) *Specialist companies* are those which underwrite one type of insurance business only, e.g., life companies, engineering insurance companies.

(b) *Composite companies* are those which underwrite several types of business.

(c) *Tariff companies* are those which are members of an association which governs the activities of its members by laying down minimum premium levels (hence the word tariff) and the form of policy wordings. The only rating association remaining is the Fire Offices' Committee (FOC) which governs fire insurance and is discussed later.

(d) *Non-tariff or independent companies* are those which operate in the same market as the tariff companies, but decide on their own policy wordings and premium levels. In practice they largely follow the tariff wordings and premium levels, but allow a discount for the better risk.

5D4. Industrial life assurance companies

Many of these companies are proprietary companies whose activities are controlled by the Industrial Assurance and Friendly Societies Acts.

Premiums are collected weekly or monthly on industrial business but they usually transact ordinary branch life business (OB) also (premiums are collected every two months or less frequently, usually quarterly, half-yearly or yearly or, if monthly, by banker's order or direct debit).

The limit of £1000 applying to Friendly Societies' policies does not apply to industrial life assurance companies who can issue policies for larger amounts.

5D5. Collecting friendly societies

These societies are run on a mutual basis and are formed by registration under the Friendly Societies Acts. They transact industrial life assurance and, in some cases, personal accident and sickness covers (see chapter 4).

While some of these societies are nationally known names, the majority operate within the area of their registered office.

Their growth arose out of the Industrial Revolution when the industrial worker required funeral benefits, at least, and these societies provided small policies with the premiums being collected weekly and therefore at a cost the worker could afford, for example, 1d. per week. Levels of cover and premiums have now risen to keep pace with the needs of society and the large home service insurers of today grew from these small beginnings. Friendly Societies can issue life assurances up to £1000 sum assured plus bonuses.

5D6. Captive insurance companies

Captive insurance is a method of transacting risk transfer which has become more common in recent years among the large national and international companies. The parent company forms a subsidiary company to underwrite certain of its insurable risks. The main incentives are to obtain the full benefit of the group's risk control techniques by paying premiums based on its own experience, avoidance of the direct insurers' overheads and obtaining a lower overall risk premium level by purchasing re-insurance at lower cost than that required by the conventional or direct insurer.

All direct insurers only retain a portion of many risks and reinsure or insure again the portion which is above their financial ability to retain. As the direct or commercial market insurer has all the procuration and survey costs to bear, the net cost of reinsurance is substantially less than the cost of direct insurance. Hence, the captive company can have access to the lower cost reinsurance market and, through the proportion of the risk retained, still have the advantages to the group of self-insurance for that amount of risk. The premiums paid to the captive company are allowable against corporation tax, although in America the IRS (the US equivalent of our Inland Revenue) has disallowed such premiums where the captive transacts no business from risks created outside the parent company.

Several captives now transact business from other sources, and many captives are operated from offshore tax havens such as Bermuda and Guernsey in order to obtain additional savings through taxation concessions in these areas.

5D7. Reinsurance companies

We have seen earlier that the principal function of insurance was to accept the transfer of risk from the public. In a similar way, the insurers may find some of the risks transferred to them too onerous, and they in turn will *re*-insure the amount above the limit of retention which they can afford to carry.

A very large international market has developed and many companies and groups (the reinsurers) specialise in accepting the transfer of this surplus or excess insurance from the companies who initially accepted the transfer from the public.

5D8. Mutual indemnity associations

Mutual indemnity associations differ from mutual companies in that the companies will accept business from the public at large, whereas an indemnity association originally would only accept business from members of a particular trade. Over the years many of the associations have had to accept business from members of the public in order to have greater financial stability and spread of risk and have been reformed as mutual or proprietary companies.

The true mutual indemnity associations grew out of trade associations and are common pools into which members of a particular trade contribute, and from which they can make a claim when necessary. The associations were formed because members of a particular trade felt that the cost of commercial insurance was too high relative to their particular claims experience, or that they had an insurance need which was not being met by the commercial market at that time.

Examples of trades which had such associations at one time were pharmacists, farmers, furniture manufacturers and shipowners. Sometimes there were a number of associations within a trade, with each one underwriting business from a fairly local area, e.g., farmers within one county or part of a county.

Contributions were made to the fund on the basis of tonnage or value and, in bad years, the members would be called upon to make additional contributions to keep the fund solvent.

Most of these associations have now been taken over by the normal insurance market, but there is still a very healthy marine market in this area. Their survival is probably due to the fact that they are the largest and longest established and were thus not under the same financial strain as other trade mutuals.

5D8A. Protecting and indemnity associations

The best known form of mutual indemnity associations are the Protecting and Indemnity Associations (or P and I Clubs). These marine associations or clubs insure liabilities for cargo, liabilities to crew, to passengers, and to third parties, including one-quarter of the shipowner's liability for damage done to another ship in collision, as the shipowner's hull policy only covers three-quarters of such liability.

5D9. Self-insurance

As an alternative to purchasing insurance in the market, or as an adjunct to it where the first layer or proportion of a claim is not insured in the commercial market, some public bodies and large industrial concerns set aside funds to meet insurable losses. As the risk is retained within the organisation, there is no market transaction of buying and selling, but such arrangements have an overall effect on the funds of the market in general and on premium levels where the organisation is carrying the first layer (excess or deductible).

These organisations have made decisions to self-insure because they feel they are large enough financially to carry such losses, and because the cost to them, by way of transfers to the fund, is lower than commercial premium levels as they are saving the insurer's administration costs and profit.

The reader should note the difference between 'self-insurance' where a conscious decision is made to create a fund, and 'non-insurance' where either no conscious decision is made at all, or where no fund is created.

Self-insurance schemes, while having certain advantages, also have some serious disadvantages.

5D9A. Advantages of self-insurance

The advantages of such a scheme may be summarized as follows:

(a) premiums should be lower as there are no costs in respect of broker's commission, insurers' administration and profit margins;

(b) interest on the investment of the fund belongs to the insured. This can be used to increase the fund or to reduce future premium contributions;

(c) the insured's premium costs are not increased due to the adverse claims experience of other firms;

(d) there is a direct incentive to reduce and control the risk of loss;

(e) no disputes will arise with insurers over claims;

(f) as the decision to self-insure is likely to be limited to large organisations, they will already have qualified insurance personnel on their staff to administer the fund;

(g) the profits from the fund accrue to the insured.

5D9B. Disadvantages of self-insurance

The drawbacks to self-insurance arrangements are as follows:

(a) a catastrophic loss, however remote, could occur, wiping out the fund and perhaps forcing the organisation into liquidation;

(b) while the organisation may be able to pay for any individual loss, the aggregate effect of several losses in one year could have the same effect as one catastrophic loss, particularly in the early years after formation of the fund;

(c) capital has to be tied up in short term, easily realisable investments which may not provide as good a yield as the better spread of investments available to an insurance company;

(d) it may be necessary to increase the number of insurance staff employed at an extra cost;

(e) the technical advice of insurers on risk prevention would be lost. The insurers' surveyors would have a wider experience over many firms and different trades, and this knowledge could be advantageous to the insured;

(f) the claims statistics of the organisation will be derived from too narrow a base for predictions to be made with confidence as to future claims costs;

(g) there may be criticism from shareholders and other departments:

(i) at the transfer of large amounts of capital to create the fund and at the cost to dividends that year, and

(ii) at the low yield on the investment of the fund compared with the yield obtainable if that amount of capital were invested in the production side of the organisation;

(h) in times of financial pressure, there may be a temptation to borrow from the fund, thus defeating the security which it had created;

(i) pressure may be brought to bear on the managers of the fund, to pay losses which are outside the cover (i.e., make *ex gratia* payments), with the resultant depletion of the fund for its legitimate purposes, and thus making statistical analysis more difficult;

(j) the basic principle of insurance, that of spreading the risk (see chapter 4), is defeated;

(k) the contributions made to the fund do not qualify as a charge against corporation tax, whereas premium payments are allowable.

5D10. The State

The State also acts as an insurer, as under the National Insurance Acts all employed persons must contribute to the National Insurance Scheme. The provisions of the National Insurance Scheme are dealt with in chapter 9.

5E. Transaction of business at Lloyd's
5E1. The Room

The underwriting room is a large hall with a gallery, 120 feet by 340 feet. Marine, motor and aviation business is transacted on the ground floor and non-marine business generally on the gallery. Underwriters and their staffs sit at 'boxes' each with a number and the Lloyd's brokers negotiate their contracts there. The Room at Lloyd's is the only place in this country where there is a recognized insurance market in the accepted sense of the word as described in the first paragraph of this chapter.

5E2. Transaction of business

It was mentioned previously, and shown in the diagram of the insurance market, that only Lloyd's brokers may place insurance at Lloyd's. When requested to place insurance at Lloyd's, the Lloyd's broker will prepare 'a slip'.

5E2A.The slip
This is a sheet of paper containing details of the risk to be insured. It will show:

—name of insured;
—property to be insured;
—period of cover required;
—sums insured or limits of liability;
—inception date of cover;
—special conditions to be incorporated;
—perils or type of cover required;
—expected premium.

5E2B.Underwriting
The broker will take the slip to an underwriter who specializes in this class of business with a view to him accepting the lead or first proportion of the risk. Discussions on other aspects of the risk e.g. claims experience, will take place and the underwriter may feel obliged to amend some of the terms on the slip before he can accept, e.g., the rate of premium or the conditions. Once agreement on terms has been reached the underwriter will stamp and initial the slip for his syndicate's proportion which he wishes to accept. This proportion may be very low, say 5%, and the broker will proceed to other underwriters until 100% is underwritten. If the broker establishes a good 'lead', other underwriters will accept the terms of the leading underwriter, otherwise the broker has to start again on the new terms.

Each underwriter will record details of the risk underwritten for his own records.

5E2C.Policy Signing Office
When the slip is complete the broker returns to his office and has the policy prepared in accordance with the slip. The policy and slip are then submitted to Lloyd's Policy Signing Office where the policy is checked with the slip and signed on behalf of all syndicates. Accounts are prepared monthly for the syndicates and brokers from the data recorded at the Policy Signing Office.

5E2D.Claims
The Lloyd's broker also provides a service to his client in the settlement of claims. In the case of marine claims he negotiates with the staff of a central office called Lloyd's Underwriters' Claims Office, and for non-marine claims he negotiates directly with the syndicates' claims officials at the boxes in 'The Room'.

5E3.Other functions of Lloyd's
5E3A.Lloyd's intelligence and other services
It will be recalled from chapter 3 that Edward Lloyd started to give shipping news in his coffee shop some 300 years ago. This service has been increased many fold so that today Lloyd's is the leading source of shipping information in the world. Information is received daily from all over the world by the Intelligence Department which distributes the information through various publications:

(a) *Lloyd's List* is a daily newspaper dealing with matters of general interest to shipowners and others with maritime interests. It also reports marine and aviation accidents, arrivals and departures of merchant shipping throughout the world, together with details of ships due to arrive or in dock at selected UK ports.

(b) *Lloyd's Shipping Index* is published Monday to Friday inclusive and lists ocean going ships alphabetically showing type of vessel, owner, flag, classification society, year of build, gross and net tonnage, current voyage and last reported position.

(c) *Lloyd's Loading List,* is published weekly and its monthly supplement *Cargo by Air* provides exporters with a valuable guide to cargo carrying services.

(d) *Lloyd's Law Reports* specialize in shipping, insurance, aviation and commercial cases heard in the English, Scottish, Commonwealth and United States Courts.

Other publications are *Lloyd's Calendar* (a handbook on Lloyd's), *Lloyd's Survey Handbook* and *Lloyd's Weekly Casualty Reports.*

Casualty Reports are prepared daily for all sections of the market and displayed on notice boards in 'The Room'.

Note Lloyd's Register of Shipping, which is a detailed register of survey details of ships, is not published by Lloyd's although members of the Committee of Lloyd's serve on the Committee of Lloyd's Register of Shipping.

5E3B.Data processing services
These, in addition to processing data from the Policy Signing Office, provide data processing facilities to other departments and other market organisations.

5E3C.Lloyd's agents
Lloyd's agents are situated in the leading ports and areas of the world and are the source of much of the information published. They also conduct surveys and arrange for surveys to be carried out in connection with losses and, if appointed as claims-settling agents, they can settle claims abroad. At present there are in the region of 1300 Lloyd's agents and sub-agents throughout the world.

5F.Organisation of insurance companies
In order to appreciate how an insurance company operates, it is helpful to look at the organisation from two particular aspects: (a) the personnel and (b) the geographical organisation.

5F1.The personnel There is no uniformity of practice or of titles from one company to another, so that the terminology and structure of an individual company may not coincide with figure 5/2 but all of these functions will be performed under some title or other.

Figure 5/2. Organisation of a typical composite company

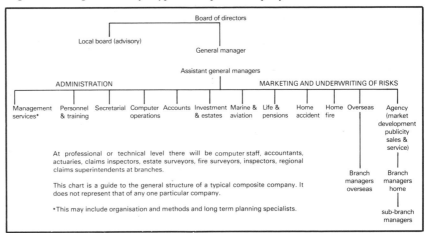

5F1A.Board of directors The function of the Board is to formulate the overall plan of operation of the company in the best interests of the owners – the shareholders – taking into account the interests of policyholders, staff, the public and the effect of market competition.

An examination of the composition of an insurance company's board will show a blend of talent with some titled persons to add prestige to the company and for the benefit of their experience in other business pursuits, prominent people from the industrial and commercial world for the benefit of their expertise, and perhaps one or two of the company's general managers for their insurance expertise.

5F1B.Local boards of directors Some companies have Boards of Directors attached to leading branch offices. These are non-executive directors and are appointed to promote the interests of the company locally and to give advice on local affairs to the branch manager.

5F1C.General managers The chief general manager is the chief executive of the company, and he will be assisted by a deputy and several assistants depending upon the size of the company. Each assistant will have a particular area of responsibility, and some of the administrative and underwriting managers shown on the chart may have assistant general manager status.

5F1D.Corporate planning manager The activities and costs of a large insurance company are now so vast that many of them have set up departments of specialists, e.g., organisation and methods staff, statisticians and economists, to advise on the changes in plan which will be necessary in the future. In this way it is hoped that the company can cope with change, and progress smoothly in a rapidly changing world.

5F1E.Company secretary The responsibilities of the company secretary are those of the administration of the organisation as a registered company and ensuring that the company complies with company and insurance company law.

5F1F.Investment manager In any large insurance company the reserves will amount to several millions of pounds, and this vast fund must be invested for security and income. In chapter 2 the investment portfolios of British companies were summarized. If long term business is transacted, the company must have an actuary to meet the legal requirements and he may be the investment manager or the life manager, perhaps with assistant general manager status.

The functions of the other personnel shown on the chart is fairly clear from their titles.

5F2.Geographical organisation The geographical organisation of a typical company is shown in figure 5/3.

5F2A.Executive head office These are usually situated in London although there are head offices in Norwich, Liverpool, Kendal, Perth, Glasgow and Edinburgh. Some companies maintain complete head offices in London, but because of the high cost of office space and salaries in London and difficulties in communication, many companies have moved the general administrative and underwriting work to a second head office in the provinces. These companies maintain only departments essential to London and small underwriting sections in the city.

Figure 5/3. Insurance company organisation – geographical

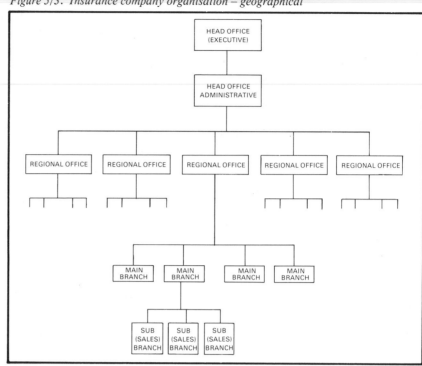

5F2B. Administrative head office

The main burden of management and underwriting is carried out here, usually in the provinces where costs are lower. The computer centre is likely to be outside London for better telecommunications.

5F2C. Regional offices

Some companies operate on a partially decentralised system (see later) where certain zonal or regional offices have underwriting authority for branches within their region.

5F2D. Main branches

These branches are responsible for initial underwriting within their area and that of their sub-branches. They are also responsible for claims handling (unless taken over by a regional office) and mainly for sales promotion.

5F2E. Sub-branches

The prime purpose of a sub-branch is sales promotion in its area.
    Not all companies operate with regional offices and this is discussed below.

5F3. Decentralisation of authority

The operational organisation of an insurance company can range from complete centralisation of all decision making at head office, to complete decentralisation with branches having wide ranging powers within broad guidelines. Between these two extremes is the regional system, whereby certain main centres are given substantial authority on underwriting and claims for the branches within the region.

5F3A. Centralisation

When a company is centralised all underwriting, claims, policy drafting, renewals and accounts work is handled from head office with the branches merely being sales outlets.
    Some advantages of centralisation are:
    (*a*) uniformity of policy, practice and routine;
    (*b*) most economic use of mechanised methods;
    (*c*) fewer experts required with a resultant saving in salaries;
    (*d*) branches relieved of routine work and can then concentrate on selling.
    Some disadvantages are:
    (*a*) the system is often run from an area of high salary, building and rating costs, e.g. London;
    (*b*) poor service can result from the administration being remote from the customer;
    (*c*) excessive power in a few hands. Dictatorial attitudes can develop in underwriting to the detriment of the company;
    (*d*) lack of promotion prospects for most of the staff.

5F3B. Decentralisation

Under this system each main branch is responsible for its own underwriting, policy drafting and claims.
    Some advantages of decentralisation are:
    (*a*) local officials will best understand local conditions;
    (*b*) good local service is possible;
    (*c*) branch staff become more knowledgeable by having to make decisions;

(*d*) brings democracy to the underwriting policy of the company;

(*e*) creates better staff morale by providing more chances of promotion to the higher grades of post required at the branches.

Some disadvantages are:

(*a*) many experts will be required, with a higher salary bill as a result;

(*b*) branches inundated with routine work, instead of concentrating on selling which is their main function;

(*c*) wasted effort in trying to make each branch expert in everything;

(*d*) divergence of practice is likely to develop between branches and this can be embarrassing if it becomes known to the public. It can also lead to misleading statistics for the company nationally.

Few companies are either completely centralised or completely decentralised and in the 1960s there was a general shift to a half-way house by way of a regional system.

5F3C. Regional system

Under this system the country was divided into, say, 10 regions and the principal branch became the regional office. It took over the underwriting, policydrafting and claims work from head office or the branches depending upon the system in force before. In this way an attempt was made to remove most of the disadvantages of both systems, while retaining many of the advantages of both systems.

In the latter part of the 1970s the tendency appeared to be to remove some of the authority from main branches to regional offices and from regional offices to head office. While this may appear to be a backward step it must be seen in the light of technological change and the greater capabilities of the computer as a labour-saving device on the one hand, and on the other, the need to increase sales volume in order to achieve the best use of those facilities where costs cannot be reduced. The present scene appears to indicate the closure of some sub-offices; withdrawal of routine work from some main branches to make them sales offices only; and removal of routine work on underwriting, endorsements and claims to the central computer, often by means of teleprinters and visual display units (VDUs) at regional offices.

5G. Insurance organisations
5G1. Organisations of intermediaries

Up to 1977 there were four organisations representing insurance brokers, the Corporation, the Association, the Federation and the Lloyd's Insurance Brokers' Association. As mentioned earlier these interests are now represented and governed by one body.

5G1A. British Insurance Brokers' Association (BIBA)

Some 3800 insurance broking businesses have already become members of BIBA and many more may be expected to join, provided they meet the requirements of the Registration Council (chapter 7). The activities of BIBA include the promotion of their views on proposed legislation and on harmonization of insurance practice within the EEC, providing research services, nominating members to sit on joint committees, encouraging the training of new entrants to the broking profession, providing a forum for discussion on various classes of insurance, on taxation and accountancy problems, public relations and consumer credit.

5G1B. Institute of Insurance Consultants

This institute was formed to 'organise, represent and enhance the status of the professional insurance consultant'. It is for the intermediary who has not registered as an insurance broker.

5G2. Organisation of Insurers

It will be apparent from a study of this chapter that there are many different interests among insurers and their intermediaries, and a study of chapter 4 will have shown that these insurers have many and varied interests over many types of insurance. It is only natural that over the years several central associations have become established to represent common interests among insurers. A summary of the activities of the more important of their associations follows, but it should be noted that this is not an exhaustive list.

✳ 5G2A. The British Insurance Association (BIA)

The BIA represents over 325 insurance companies transacting some 95 per cent of the worldwide business of the British insurance company market.

The BIA sets out to represent the interests of its members by:

— acting as a single authoritative voice for members and as a channel of communications between them and the government, financial organisations and the bodies which seek to consult the insurance market;

— conducting a public relations programme designed to improve public appreciation and understanding of insurance;

— studying a wide range of technical subjects on behalf of members;

— operating a system whereby complaints against member companies can be investigated at senior level within the company concerned.

Examples of its work in these areas either recently or currently as ongoing programmes are:

(*a*) submissions to the Pearson Committee, i.e., the Royal Commission on Civil Liability and Compensation for Personal Injury;

(*b*) submissions, jointly with Life Associations (see later), to the Commission to Review the Functioning of Financial Institutions under the chairmanship of Sir Harold Wilson;

(*c*) consultation with the Inland Revenue on various aspects of taxation;

(*d*) discussions with accounting bodies on accounting standards;

(*e*) representing the interest of members at the drafting stage of law reform reports and statutes such as the Policyholders' Protection Act 1975, the Insurance Companies Act 1974 and the Insurance Brokers' (Registration) Act 1977;

(*f*) research into vehicle repair methods and costs at the Motor Insurance Repair Research Centre at Thatcham, operated jointly with Lloyd's, motor engineers' units for vehicle repair at various places throughout England, and risk statistics in the areas of motor insurance, employers' liability insurance and household risks;

(*g*) public relations through press advertising, schools literature, films, radio and TV interviews and press conferences mostly through the work of the BIA's regional committees and officers;

(*h*) consultations and conferences with the Health and Safety Executive on industrial safety;

(*i*) consultation with various interested parties within the EEC on the drafting of EEC Directives relating to insurance.

5G3. Marine insurance organisations
5G3A. Lloyd's Underwriters' Association

This Association acts officially for marine underwriters at Lloyd's in all technical matters relating to their business. Its membership comprises all Lloyd's marine underwriters and the Association concerns itself with various underwriting and general administrative problems which arise in Lloyd's marine market. The Association also keeps its members advised of all developments and other pertinent information that is likely to have some bearing upon the underwriting of marine business at Lloyd's.

The Association acts in close liaison with the Institute of London Underwriters and Liverpool Underwriters' Association, and appoints Lloyd's representatives to serve on various joint committees, which deliberate upon problems that are common both to the Lloyd's and company marine market.

5G3B. The Institute of London Underwriters

This is a forum for the company marine insurance underwriters. The Institute operates a policy signing office similar to that in operation at Lloyd's. In order to simplify the placing of business among various companies and in claims settlements, it is desirable that all policies covering the one risk have similar clauses and wordings. The standard clauses used by its members, known as 'Institute Clauses' are now used by the British market as a whole. It is these clauses which are attached to the MAR form.

5G3C. Liverpool Underwriters' Association

This Association represents the interests of marine insurers, brokers and loss adjusters operating in the Liverpool marine insurance market. It provides a shipping intelligence service and produces statistics on maritime losses.

5G4. Organisations associated with fire and fire insurance

These organisations are all concerned with protection against fire damage, or with the transaction of fire insurance, although there is some interdependency.

5G4A. Fire Offices' Committee (FOC)

This is the association of many of the leading company fire insurers in Great Britain. It forms the 'tariff' group of companies whose aim is to pool statistical information and so obtain as sound a statistical footing as possible on which to base rating requirements for the future. It also publishes for its members a very detailed scale of minimum (but not maximum) rates for many types of trade, thus establishing a sound economical base to the fire insurance market. As in marine insurance, it is desirable to have standard policy wordings in the fire market where so many risks are shared and the FOC prepares such wordings for their members.

There is close liaison between the FOC and the 'non-tariff' or 'independent' offices and Lloyd's.

It is sometimes argued that a monopoly has been created in the UK fire market, as the independents and Lloyd's often use the tariff rating structure with a small discount. In spite of a recommendation several years ago by the Monopolies Commission that the rating part of the FOC should be disbanded, it is still functioning.

The reason that this has been allowed to continue is probably due to the fact that the tariff rating structure ensures a solid financial base to the market, while the existence of the independents (a number of them are among the largest ten companies) and Lloyd's ensure that the tariff companies must not charge more than a fair and economic premium or they will be undercut.

The FOC also draft rules and recommendations for the construction of buildings, fire doors, fire protection systems, and the operation of various processes, e.g., paint spraying, storage of oils, to ensure a minimum standard of fire protection.

5G4B. Lloyd's Underwriters' Fire and Non-Marine Association

This association deals with matters affecting the fire and non-marine market at Lloyd's. Its activities are not nearly so extensive as those of the FOC.

5G4C. Fire Protection Association

This is an association run jointly by the FOC and industry and specializing in research, education and advice on fire protection matters for industry, commerce and the public. It publishes journals giving (*a*) reports on important and unusual fires for the layman and (*b*) reports and research reports for the scientist, engineer and expert.

5G4D. Fire Insurers' Research and Testing Organisation (FIRTO)

This association runs a testing establishment to determine the reaction of material, building materials and fire extinguishment techniques under simulated fire conditions. The organisation works closely with the Government Building Research Establishment with whom they previously formed one organisation, the Joint Fire Research Organisation.

5G4E. Central Fire Liaison Panels

These panels were formed by the BIA, the Confederation of British Industry (CBI) and the local fire brigades to provide on-the-spot advice to local industry on their fire protection problems and to provide education material locally. The Fire Protection Association has now taken over the rôle of the BIA in relation to the panels.

5G5. Life assurance associations
5G5A. Life Offices' Association and Associated Scottish Life Offices

The Life Offices' Association with its sister association in Scotland, the Associated Scottish Life Offices, is the central association for ordinary life assurance in the United Kingdom. The Association maintains a close watch on legislative and other developments affecting the common interests of its members at home and overseas, and is frequently in consultation with the various government departments and organisations concerned.

Among its many other activities the Association collects and disseminates statistical and other information relating to the business, and in recent years has sponsored a collective public relations campaign.

5G5B. Industrial Life Offices' Association

The main purposes of this Association are to maintain the principles, practice and business of industrial (home-service) life assurance and to foster the prestige and goodwill of the industry. Its membership includes both companies and collecting friendly societies.

In 1949 it became necessary to oppose the threat to nationalise industrial life assurance. A plebiscite held by the offices established that the majority of those employed in the industry were opposed to nationalisation. It was accordingly decided to conduct a campaign by forming local committees of employees throughout the country. Over 400 such committees were set up.

To guide and control these committees a Central Information Office was established in London and regional information officers were appointed at a number of centres throughout the country.

When the immediate threat of nationalisation receded, the campaign was changed to one of prestige and goodwill. This campaign still continues and the local committees, supported by press advertising, provide the impetus. Their principal activity is the holding of annual luncheons to which representatives of the local civic, commercial and professional life are invited. The committees also arrange talks on home-service insurance to other organisations and co-operate with the local press on matters concerning the business.

5G6. Accident engineering and aviation insurance organisations
5G6A. Accident Offices' Association

This is an association of accident insurance companies transacting business in the United Kingdom or Ireland. The Association provides a meeting place for the discussion of matters of interest to its members. From the introduction of compulsory third party motor insurance, and particularly since the war, there have been an increasing number of occasions when it has been necessary for all accident insurers to consider common problems.

The Accident Offices' Association (Overseas) corresponds to the Fire Offices' Committee (Foreign), and it is concerned with the considerable portfolio of tariff accident insurance business transacted overseas by its members. The Association provides the necessary secretarial assistance for, among others, The Motor Conference, which is a forum where technical motor insurance matters are discussed by companies and Lloyd's.

5G6B. Lloyd's Motor Underwriters' Association

This Association deals with matters affecting the business of motor insurance at Lloyd's. Membership comprises those syndicates at Lloyd's who specialise in motor insurance and most have adopted individual titles by which they are known and recognized.

5G6C. Mutual Insurance Companies' Association

The Association was constituted for the purpose of considering matters connected with the business of its members and the taking of such measures as may be thought expedient for the protection and furtherance of their interests. The stimulus to its formation (in 1942) was provided by the necessity for mutual companies to give evidence, independently of the companies generally, before the Beveridge Committee, whose function was to enquire into social insurance issues, the most important of which from the insurance market point of view was that concerning industrial injury provided for under the then existing Workmen's Compensation Acts.

In the main the members of the Association are concerned primarily or exclusively with employers' liability insurance, and their activities as a rule are, in addition, confined to specific sections of industry.

5G6D. Aviation Insurance Offices' Association

This Association is designed to promote, advance and protect the interests of insurance companies transacting aviation insurance business, that is to say, the business of effecting contracts of insurance for the purpose of insuring owners or hirers of any aircraft against loss of or damage to or arising out of or in connection with the use of the aircraft including third party risks, or insurance of air cargo (either against loss to the consignor or the liability of the carrier); or such other types of insurance associated with aviation as the members may designate from time to time. Among its objects it ensures joint action where necessary to draw up standard policy wordings and clauses in co-operation with other insurance interests concerned with aviation insurance.

5G6E. Lloyd's Aviation Underwriters' Association

This Association represents the interests of Lloyd's aviation market. At first membership was confined to the underwriters of specialist aviation syndicates, but is now open to the underwriters of any syndicate underwriting aviation business.

The Association has published a book of policy forms and clauses for use in aviation business, and this is periodically brought up to date as new forms are introduced and amendments made to existing forms and clauses.

5G6F. International associations

Among the international associations there are the International Union of Marine Insurance, the International Union of Aviation Insurers, and the International Credit Insurance Association.

5G7. Motor Insurers' Bureau (MIB)

As was seen earlier the Road Traffic Acts require vehicle users to be insured for liability for personal injuries to other road users. The intention is to ensure that all injury victims will get compensation for their injuries caused by negligent drivers. However, the injured party would have no recovery or little likelihood of one in the following circumstances:

(a) where the driver has no insurance policy;

(b) where the driver and therefore his insurer is untraced, i.e., the hit and run case;

(c) where the insurer goes into liquidation (in this case only a very small part of the claim is likely to be met and that may take years to complete).

The MIB was established in 1946 by arrangement between motor insurers and the government to create a central fund maintained by the insurers, whereby victims would get compensation in the instances cited, provided they could establish their claims to the satisfaction of the normal rules of civil law. It is then left to the MIB to try to recover from the driver, but this is seldom possible.

Another function of the MIB is to guarantee, to foreign governments, performance by British motor insurers under the terms of the insurance certificates issued by them for foreign travel.

5G8. Chartered Insurance Institute (CII)

The main purpose is to ensure an adequate education for its members and to enable them to sit the Institute's examinations. After passing these examinations and completing a satisfactory period of practical experience, members can apply to be elected Associates (ACII) and later after further examinations and experience Fellows (FCII) of the Chartered Insurance Institute. Education for these examinations is provided by correspondence courses run by the Institute's own Tuition Service or by commercial organisations, and by the various college courses run by local authorities on either a part-time or full-time basis. The Institute runs a College of Insurance for short, full-time courses on a wide range of topics. Membership is open to all persons engaged in or employed in insurance and so is open to company personnel, brokers, and Lloyd's personnel. There are numerous local institutes throughout the country and meetings are held frequently, either on administrative matters or in the form of talks on subjects of interest, usually with invited speakers.

6. Risk management

6A.The concept of risk management

So far we have looked at the nature of risk itself, identified those risks which can be transferred to the insurance market, plotted the historical development of insurance, outlined the main classes of insurance and described the insurance market place. The emphasis has been firmly on insurance, not unreasonably so as this whole book is concerned with introducing the reader to the business of insurance.

What we must do now, however, is to try to locate insurance in the overall concept of the management of risk. There is much more to the management of risk than simply buying insurance for those risks which happen to be insurable. Over the past three decades we have seen a marked development in what has become known as 'Risk Management'. Techniques have been developed and refined which allow for risks to be identified, their effect evaluated and the most efficient means of control discovered. In short we could say that risk management is the identification, evaluation and economic control of those risks which threaten the assets or earning capabilities of an organisation. When you progress to the Fellowship of the CII you will see that one of the optional subjects there is in fact 'Risk Management'. An entire subject, and course book, is devoted to the concept, so clearly there is much more to it than can easily be confined within this chapter.

What we will endeavour to do is to locate our current knowledge of insurance within the overall picture of risk management and then move on to look at the key components of our definition, i.e. identification, evaluation and control.

6A1.The risk management process

Risk management takes a far broader view of the problems posed by risk than does insurance. This is the first important point to grasp as we try to discover the nature of risk management. Rather than being limited to insurable risks, of the form we have already studied, risk management starts at a far more fundamental level and asks the basic question: to what risks is this organisation exposed? It moves on from there to evaluate the likely impact on the organisation by looking at both severity and frequency. Having identified the risk and evaluated it, risk management techniques are then applied to decide how this identified risk could be best controlled.

This process is shown in diagram form in figure 6/1 where we can see a simple representation of the various stages of risk management.

Figure 6/1. The risk management process

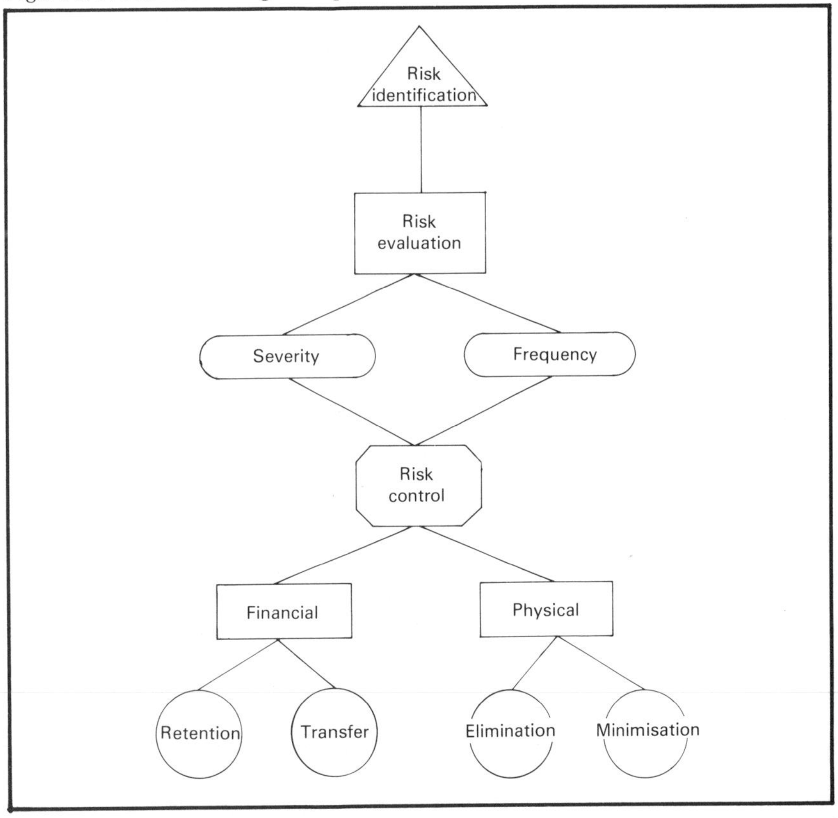

We can see from this diagram that the financial transfer of risk will be the stage in the process involving insurance. Insurance was defined earlier in this book as a risk transfer mechanism and it is in this capacity that it relates to risk management. (Insurance is, however, not the only form of financial risk transfer, as we shall see later.)

Insurance then, is one part of the risk management process. This statement sets insurance in perspective in relation to the overall concept of risk management. It is not intended to demean the rôle played by insurance but simply to establish the fact that risk management is not a part or sub-set of insurance. Insurance is, in fact, a sub-set of risk management.

Viewed this way it is easy to see why the concept of risk management was not met with overwhelming enthusiasm by those engaged in insurance, in the early days. Risk management was viewed by many, and perhaps still is to a certain extent, as an attack on the part insurance had always played in the management of risk. As the benefits of risk management began to be experienced, a number of insurers and insurance brokers started to embrace the concept and there are now a large number of insurers and brokers who offer comprehensive risk management services. Indeed many of the advances in risk management methodology are attributable to these firms.

6B. Risk management methodology

Let us now take the three main steps of identification, evaluation and control and expand on each one in turn.

6B1. Risk identification

Risk management takes the view that a firm is exposed to risk in a variety of ways and any one such way may cause financial loss. Risk is viewed therefore in its widest sense, and not limited to those risks that can be insured. Steps are taken, using established risk indentification aids, to highlight all areas where a company is likely to suffer. The advantage of having a risk manager identify exposure areas is, in the main, that he is a specialist at his job and is not limited to one particular function of the company. An engineer may be able to identify risks in his area, the lawyer in his and the marketing man in his but the risk manager, while not being a specialist in other disciplines has the capability of overseeing all their activities.

The task of risk identification is of course a daunting one. Just think of a large factory complex, shopping centre, airport or any other large risk. Where would you begin the job of identifying risk? There must be some structure to your approach and this structure is to be found in a number of risk identification techniques.

6B1A. Risk identification techniques

Before starting any risk identification it is essential to carry out some kind of physical inspection. This may simply take the form of a brief walk over the plant to complement what you may have read in company publicity material or heard from managers at the factory. This initial step helps in giving a 'feel' for the place and may later direct your formal risk identification in one way or another. Having done this, one or more of the following may be a helpful aid to identifying risk.

(a) *Organisational Charts*. These charts will show the basic organisational structure of the plant or of an entire company. It will show the relationship between and among different personnel. It could, for example, highlight weaknesses in organisational structure which could cause problems for the risk manager. It may be that the chart highlights the fact that the works manager has a lengthy process to complete in the reporting of accidents. The risk manager may well decide that the work involved could be a positive disincentive to effective reporting of accidents and near accidents by the works manager. This could lead to a streamlining of the system and hence more effective information reaching the risk manager quickly.

(b) *Flow Chart*. A flow chart is particularly useful in companies where the system of manufacture or production involves materials 'flowing' through a process. Figure 6/2 illustrates a system where a product 'X' is manufactured. The flow shows that two items of raw material 'A' and 'B' arrive in quantities of 100 and 200 respectively, 'A' by road from a subsidiary and 'B' by rail. The two ingredients are processed in plants 1 and 2 and as a result in the case of 'B' a by-product 'C' is produced. The resultant ingredients are processed in plant 3 and then are added to in plant 4 before finally producing two sets of finished product 'X'.

A chart such as this shows the flow of the operation and can highlight problems which would be caused by unforeseen events. For example, if plant 3 was put out of commission by, say, fire or explosion then the risk manager would have to consider the effects of this on the operation; how will the subsidiary which processes 'A' be affected? Can the order for 'B' be cancelled? Will there be a breach of contract for the sale of by-product 'C'? What is the effect on the subsidiary which uses by-product 'F'? These and other questions arise simply from looking at the chart and will prompt the risk manager to seek answers.

Figure 6/2. Risk identification flow chart

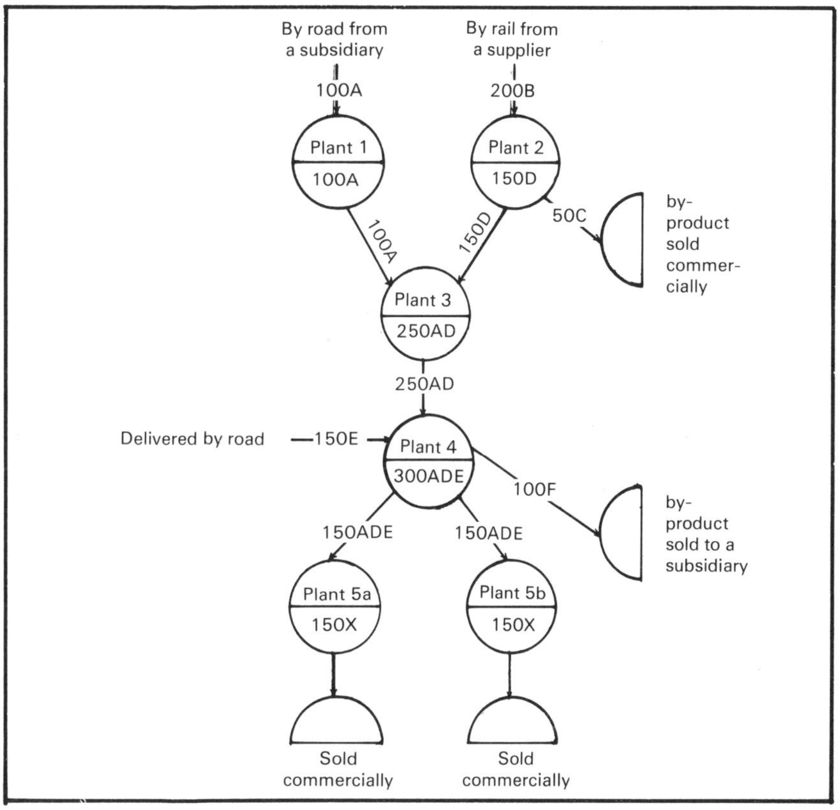

(c) *Check List.* Another form of risk identification involves the risk manager in asking a number of questions about each item of plant. For example, he may firstly list the main areas of activity within a factory complex and then set about asking the same set of questions for each area. These questions normally revolve around the risks to which the plant could be exposed. The following exposures, or classification of risk, could be used.

Figure 6/3. Classification of risks

DIRECT	Fire, corrosion, explosion, fraud, structural defect, war.
CONSEQUENTIAL	Loss of profits following fire, following theft, inter-group dependency, strikes.
SOCIAL	Moral liability, consumer pressure.
LEGAL	Civil liabilities, statutory liabilities, contractual liabilities.
POLITICAL	Governmental intervention, sanctions, acts of foreign governments.
FINANCIAL	Inadequate inflation forecasts, incorrect marketing decisions.

This type of exercise brings some kind of structure to the risk manager's thinking on risk identification; it breaks down the task into more manageable units.

There are a large number of other techniques which can be used, including Fault Trees, Hazard Analysis, Hazard and Operability Studies, all of which aid the risk manager in identifying risk. These are very complex and are outside the scope of the present study.

6B2.Risk evaluation   The second stage in the risk management process is that of evaluating the impact of risk on the firm. Often this evaluation can be made in a qualitative manner, that is, without the use of quantitative analysis. A risk manager could, for example, study the flow chart in figure 6/2 and make certain qualitative evaluations as to the effects which specific events may have. In some cases this may be all that is possible because accurate records have not been kept and further quantitative analysis would be impossible. This kind of qualitative risk evaluation is something which benefits from experience and those involved in risk management invariably fall back on their own experience of similar events or situations in measuring the potential impact of risks.

We have already said something in chapter 1 about the quantitative evaluation of risk. Any statistical work which is done in risk evaluation will only be as good as the data which have been gathered and which formed the base of the calculation. We could say then that the statistical analysis of risk really starts with the keeping of adequate records. Only if we have these records will we be able to carry out any form of valid statistical work. One major difficulty is that these records have to be compiled before the immediate need for them arises. In other words, if a risk manager decided to self-insure the theft risk to which his premises are exposed he would want to measure the impact of the theft risk on his company. If he had not been keeping accurate records of theft losses he would find it very difficult to look back over, say, the last five years and try to remember all such incidents.

With modern computer technology, the keeping of records is much less of a burden than it used to be. Incidents can be entered on a computer file and codes used to indicate the type of incident and the plant at which it occurred. Later the file can be up-dated to show the final loss figure, the date settled and any other relevant facts. If incidents are reported regularly to the risk manager and if these reported incidents are accurately recorded, then an invaluable source of information is collected which can later be turned to the risk manager's advantage.

Not only does the computer store loss information but it can carry out appropriate statistical analysis including prediction of loss trends. However, whatever figures are produced are only 'estimates' of what may happen. In the end the risk manager must form his own judgement as to what *he* believes will happen.

6B3. Risk control

The third and final step in the risk management process shown in figure 6/1 is the control of risk. It can be seen from the diagram that this falls into two parts, physical and financial. In the end it is economic control of risk which is the objective of the risk manager. He has identified and evaluated risk only so that he can decide how best to respond to it. This final step is the important decision stage where he must use all of the information he now has in his possession to make the *best* decisions on behalf of his company.

6B3A. Physical control of risk

The picture being built up is one of an environment in which risk is invariably present in one form or another. In spite of this, life continues both on a personal as well as a business level but the pervasive nature of risk has resulted in a great deal of effort being directed at how losses can be prevented.

Loss prevention is sometimes referred to as risk reduction but we can look upon the terms as being synonymous. Our definition of risk was uncertainty of loss, and risk reduction can therefore be viewed as a means of removing some or all of this uncertainty.

The importance of loss prevention cannot be understated. In 1983 fires caused damage in Great Britain estimated at £565.6m. This is an extremely high figure and it is difficult to visualize what it actually means. The amount refers to fire damage, whether insured or not, but does not include other losses that flow from a fire such as lost profit. To try to put this figure, sometimes known as the fire waste figure, in perspective recall that in chapter 1 we saw that it amounted to £18 every single *second* of 1983.

To reduce this high fire loss figure would be commendable on its own and certainly sufficient justification for examining methods of loss prevention, but what makes these efforts all the more necessary is the fact that the loss does not end with the visible damage. Just as we noted above, fire damage results in a chain of other losses and this is true for most forms of risk.

Let us look at one risk as an example. A pure and particular risk to which almost all businesses are exposed is that of injury to employees. When an employee is injured he may succeed in legal action against his employer for compensation, and the employer will have an insurance policy to provide him with the money he requires to pay the injured employee's claim. The claim from the employee can be looked upon in the same way as the fire damage cost: it is not the end of the story. While the injured man is away from work there will be lost production, another person may have to be trained, there will have been a stoppage of production at the time of the injury, and other employees may have to act as witnesses at a court case if one ensues. The point is that if the loss could have been prevented it would have resulted in there being no injury and no consequential stream of losses. The importance of loss prevention goes beyond the individual or firm involved in the loss as the whole of society benefits from there being fewer losses in the long run.

Elimination

Many people equate loss prevention with elimination of loss. This is natural enough as one sure way of not having a loss is to eliminate the possibility altogether.

In a domestic sense this is often possible. Where a person is really concerned over the likelihood of a motor accident then he or she could sell their car and eliminate the risk. In the same way they may be alarmed in case their pet dog causes injury to neighbouring children and they could sell or otherwise dispose of the animal in order to eliminate the risk. For some risks, elimination will not be possible. No matter how worried you may be about the chip pan going on fire in the kitchen you may like chips too much to dispose of the pan. On a more serious note, you may be concerned over the possibility of fire damage to your house but you would not think of selling your house to eliminate the risk.

In the business world it is very common to be faced with problems posed by risk where elimination is not viable. There may be considerable risk attached to the building of a new factory, risks that could be eliminated if you decided not to build, but the whole organisation depends upon the new building being constructed and it is just not possible to eliminate the risk entirely.

Minimisation

These thoughts on the inability to eliminate risk lead us on to consider how best the risk or loss can be minimised. Loss prevention is therefore concerned primarily with minimising risk, or according to our definition with minimising the uncertainty of loss.

The effort of minimising losses falls into two divisions:

(*a*) *Pre-Loss Minimisation.* As we saw in chapter 5 insurance companies employ specialists who can assist individuals or firms in working out ways of minimising losses by steps taken before the adverse event has occurred. The wearing of seat belts in private cars is a good example. The essence of this pre-loss minimisation is that the effect of the loss is anticipated and steps taken to ensure that the frequency and/or severity are reduced to the minimum.

The use of guards on dangerous machinery anticipates the risk of injury to employees; the installation of extractor fans in a paint spraying booth anticipates the risks of injury to health and fire damage.

A great measure of experience is required in being able to anticipate risks and persuade people to take steps to minimize their effect. A general response to risk reduction suggestions is the statement, 'it won't happen to me!' In some cases this is often shown to be sadly inaccurate.

(*b*) *Post-Loss Minimisation.* Even after the risk has materialized and the loss taken place there are still steps that can be taken to minimise loss. The most common area where post-loss minimisation occurs is probably after fire damage. Property can often be saved from burning buildings and other property salvaged and sold in an attempt to minimise the loss.

Just as pre-loss minimisation anticipated the loss before it took place, post-loss minimisation imagines that the loss has occurred and anticipates a way in which its effect can be minimized. In this way the employment of an industrial nurse may minimize the effect of an injury. Automatic sprinkler installations will minimize the effect of fires.

6B3B. Financial control of risk

We have dealt with loss prevention and this is an arm of control but what we have not looked at are the ways in which risks can be reduced by some financial mechanism. We could divide this form of risk reduction into two categories: retention and transfer.

Retention

After identification and evaluation of the risks facing his company the risk manager may find that in an individual factory, a given level of fire loss can be expected each year. The purpose of insurance is really to transfer the unpredictable risks, but in this case there is a certain level of loss which is predictable from previous experience. If each year fire losses in aggregate vary from £100,000 upwards, then to insure this first layer of £100,000 will cost £100,000 by way of premium *plus* the insurers' overheads, commission and profit.

The insurers may allow a discount in premium of some amount if the insured carry this first £100,000 themselves, in which case the insured will retain an excess or deductible of £100,000 in aggregate per year, with an excess/deductible of say £25,000 per loss. This means that the insured will pay up to £25,000 each fire loss until a total of £100,000 is reached in any one insurance year.

The cost of these losses can be paid out of current income and charged as part of the cost of production. Alternatively, a separate fund could be set up to pay them and other risks which may be fully retained. Such a fund is called self-insurance and was discussed in chapter 5.

One development of the retention of risk has been the formation of captive insurance companies. Certain businesses are so large that they can very well insure some of their risks themselves and in this way save the element of the premiums that would otherwise go towards the insurance companies' costs and expenses. A wholly owned subsidiary is set up and some risks are passed to it and premiums paid by the parent organisation to this captive. In some cases the captive also transacts insurance for firms other than its parent and can very often become a profit maker in the same way as any other subsidiary that the parent may establish.

Captives were discussed in some detail in chapter 5 and the reader can see now how the concept of captive insurance companies fits into the overall concept of risk management. One topical point to make is that in the current 'soft' market the incentive to establish a captive has been questioned by some people. When premiums are already low it may be possible to arrange complete transfer of the risk to an insurer in the direct market, rather than go to the trouble of establishing your own insurer.

Transfer
The second method of financial risk control could be said to be those situations where the company transfers the effect of the loss to some other person or company. A company that owns property and lets it out to tenants is exposed to the risk that their property may be damaged by fire. The company can transfer this risk by writing into the contract, the lease, that the tenant is responsible for fire damage and must effect a fire insurance policy. This is looked upon as financial risk control as the owners of the property are, in a sense, paying to have the risk transferred because if they had retained the risk they could probably have charged a higher rent.

The most common form of risk transfer is by way of insurance and in chapter 2 we discussed insurance as a risk transfer mechanism. In chapter 4 the various classes of risk which can be transferred in this way were discussed.

Insurance will always be the most important method of paying for the cost of risk, but the way in which it is used is changing. From the 'insure all' practice of a few decades ago, the tendency in the next few decades will be to retain more of the high frequency, low severity risks and to retain the lower levels of more serious losses by means of deductibles or captive insurance. The insurance market will remain the means by which catastrophe risks are financed.

6C. Personal risk management

The various risk management processes which have been discussed are normally carried out in large and some medium sized companies by a risk or insurance manager (the title does not always give a good description of the nature of the work done) and his/her small team.

The individual in his personal and domestic risk situation, or the small trader with his business interests, can follow similar techniques.

Flow charts, check lists and so on can be used to identify risks, and professional advice sought on the best physical and financial tools to be used to handle them.

It is important that a conscious effort is made to study and control the risks which face us daily. Large scale retention of risk is unlikely to be financially acceptable but much can be done to arrange a more satisfactory insurance programme than would be the case without adopting such techniques.

6D. Conclusion

There is no doubt that the concept of risk management has grown considerably over recent decades. The Association of Insurance and Risk Managers in Industry and Commerce (AIRMIC) now has several hundred practising risk and insurance managers as members.

Over the foreseeable future we can look for a steady growth in the development of risk management and an increasing number of career opportunities for those with the ability to take the broad view of risk.

References
N. Crockford, *Introduction to Risk Management*, Woodhead–Faulkner.
Bannister and Bawcutt, *Practical Risk Management*, Witherby.
Greene and Serbein, *Risk Management Text and Cases*, Reston Publishing Co.

7. Government supervision

7A.The role of government supervision

Government has always taken an interest in insurance activities over the years. On occasions this supervision has amounted to direct intervention and the State provision of insurance such as with the National Insurance scheme of which more is said in chapter 9. More often the supervision has taken the form of statutes governing aspects of the transaction of insurance. In more recent years, in relation to the long history of insurance, governments have legislated to make certain forms of insurance compulsory.

Before going on to suggest why there should be any element of government supervision we will look back and trace the growth of supervision.

7A1.Historical development of supervision
7A1A.Life Assurance Companies Act 1870

Some would say that the earliest record of government intervention was possibly the Chamber of Assurances founded in 1575 whereby marine policies had to be registered. The pattern of modern supervision, however, could be said to have started in 1870 with the Life Assurance Companies Act, which made it obligatory for life assurance companies to make a deposit of £20,000 with the High Court before they could transact business. In addition detailed accounting and actuarial returns had to be made to the Board of Trade in order that the solvency, the extent to which assets exceeded liabilities, could be monitored. Similar controls were also imposed on companies transacting employers' liability insurance by the Employers' Liability Insurance Companies Act 1907.

7A1B.Assurance Companies Act 1909

By this Act the supervision of insurance business was extended beyond life assurance to fire, personal accident and bond investment. Lloyd's underwriters were exempted from the provisions of the Act provided they complied with specified requirements. This Act was the framework upon which supervision of insurance was built for half a century.

7A1C.Industrial Assurance Act 1923

The Act provided that Industrial Assurance was to be treated as a separate class of business (it has since been incorporated in later legislation) and limited its transaction to certain specified organisations. One major innovation was the establishment of an Industrial Assurance Commissioner who was to exercise the statutory powers of the Board of Trade in relation to industrial life assurance.

7A1D.Assurance Companies Act 1946

Since the passing of the 1909 Act several new classes of business had been introduced and their regulation was incorporated in this 1946 Act. Motor, aviation and transit insurances were brought within the scope of the Act, as was the more established marine business. The main reason for noting this Act is, however, the fact that it abolished the need for deposits and replaced them with a new system. Several insurance companies had found their liabilities exceeding their assets, that is, the amount they had to pay or were to pay in the future had exceeded the amount of money they had to meet these payments. In the main this was attributable to the substantial growth in motor insurance business, with not all companies who offered insurance being in a financially sound position so to do. The Assurance Companies (Winding Up) Acts 1933–35 are evidence of the need for some tightening up of insurers' financial reserves.

Solvency Margins

In place of the deposits, in the case of non-life business, companies were required to satisfy certain solvency requirements measured in terms of solvency margins. The margin related to the amount by which assets were to exceed liabilities. In brief this meant that each company had to maintain a balance between how much it had in terms of assets and how much it knew it had to pay or would be likely to pay in liabilities. The exact requirement under the 1946 Act was that each company should have (*a*) a minimum paid-up share capital of £50,000, and (*b*) assets exceeding liabilities by £50,000 or 10% of the previous year's premium income, whichever was the greater. The present position regarding solvency margins is discussed later.

7A1E. Insurance Companies Act 1958

The 1958 Act consolidated all the previous relevant statutes since 1909. The new Act introduced certain requirements relating to accounts and audits but it would only serve to confuse if we were to consider it in detail.

7A1F. Companies Act 1967

Part II of the Companies Act 1967 met the need for stronger powers that had arisen during the early sixties. A number of motor insurers had failed during this period, despite the solvency requirement, and fresh margins for non-life business were set at (*a*) a minimum paid-up share capital of £100,000, (*b*) in the first year of trading assets had to exceed liabilities by £50,000, (*c*) in subsequent trading periods assets were to exceed liabilities by £50,000 where the premium income in the previous year was not greater than £250,000 but where the premium income exceeded £250,000 the margin was to be at least 20% on the first £2,500,000 plus 10% on the balance of that income.

Regulations relating to authorisation of insurers, reinsurance requirements, management of companies, initial conduct of business, actuarial valuation of life funds and insolvency and winding up were also made. Following the collapse of the Vehicle and General Insurance Company in 1971, and the report of the Scott Committee on Property Bonds and Equity Linked Life Assurance, in 1973, came the Insurance Companies Amendment Act 1973 which introduced additional regulatory powers.

7A1G. Current position

In 1974 the Insurance Companies Act consolidated the 1958, 1967 and 1973 provisions in one statute. During the latter part of the 1970's a large volume of legislation and regulations was passed concerning various aspects of supervision.

This increase in legislation during the 1970's, particularly the latter half of the decade, is probably due to two quite different factors.

Firstly, there were a number of failures of insurance companies, and this prompted many to believe that the then current legislation lacked power in certain directions. The lack of effective supervision of insurance company operations was demonstrated in 1965 when Emil Savundra's Fire Auto and Marine Insurance Company failed. A tightening of legislation followed but in 1971 the Vehicle and General Insurance failed, leaving hundreds of thousands of motor policyholders uninsured. Further legislation ensued but it was not sufficient to prevent another failure, this time in the life field, of Nation Life in 1974. These three insurance company failures, linked with the growing move towards increased consumer protection, played a major part in encouraging Parliament to take action to increase its powers.

The second factor which promoted the growth of insurance company legislation was our involvement with the EEC. Under the 1974 Insurance Companies Act some twenty-two Statutory Instruments were passed, many of which were made to implement the terms of the EEC Non-life Establishment Directive 73/239/EEC. These Instruments, intended to bring about some harmonization of European insurance legislation, dealt with matters such as solvency margins, defining new classes of business, authorization of insurance companies, etc. In 1979 the EEC Life Establishment Directive 79/267/EEC was introduced and was followed closely by the Insurance Companies Act 1981 which consolidated much of the then existing European legislation.

One can easily see how complicated the whole area became, because of the desire to respond to the consumer orientated problems in Britain and the need to conform with and integrate European directives. Fortunately, the position was greatly clarified by the passing of the Insurance Companies Act 1982 which came into effect on 28th January 1983. This Act, supplemented by other legislation, now represents the regulatory powers as they currently apply. The particular agency of government which is concerned with the implementation of the terms of the Act is the Insurance Division of the Department of Trade and Industry under the direction of the Secretary of State for Trade and Industry.

7B. The Insurance Companies Act 1982

This new Act, in one hundred sections, consolidates without change to existing law the provisions of the Insurance Companies Act 1981. All statutory instruments made under preceding legislation continue in being and are interpreted as if they had been made under the corresponding sections of the 1982 Act. It would not be totally accurate to say that all regulatory issues are now contained within the 1982 Act as, for example, the Insurance Companies Regulations 1981 (SI 1981 No. 1654) are still current.

We must decide however, what it is necessary to know in order to gain some appreciation of the current legislative position. We will therefore outline the main provisions of the 1982 Act, making reference where it is felt necessary, to other regulations.

The one hundred sections of the Act fall into five main parts:

1. *Restriction on Carrying on Insurance Business*. This part is concerned with defining the various classes of business and with the requirements to be met by those wishing to carry on the business of insurance.

2. *Regulation of Insurance Companies*. Part Two of the Act is by far the largest, with 57 individual sections. Primarily it is concerned with financial matters such as annual accounts, actuarial investigation, winding-up and other matters.

3. *Conduct of Insurance Business*. Insurance advertisements, 'cooling-off' notices for life assurance and the disclosure by intermediaries of connections with an insurance company are some of the items dealt with by the ten sections of Part Three.

4. *Special Classes of Insurers*. These sections are concerned chiefly with Lloyd's, industrial life assurance, and companies established outside the United Kingdom.

5. *Supplementary*. Much of this final part is concerned with the criminal proceedings which would follow any breach of the Act. It also provides for the Secretary of State for Trade to make an annual report on the operation of the Act.

For our purposes we will concentrate on six main areas: Authorization, Solvency, Monitoring, Intervention, Conduct of Business and Winding-up.

7B1. Authorization

The general 'flavour' of the regulations concerning authorization is that any company wishing to transact insurance must be authorized to do so by the Department of Trade and Industry. To gain this authorization the Department must be satisfied that the applicant complies with a number of conditions as laid down in the Act and the 1981 Insurance Company Regulations. The objective is that only companies operated by 'fit and proper' persons should transact business.

In short then, the Secretary of State has the power to authorize a company to transact long term business or general business, including reinsurance. He can also restrict authorization to specific types of business.

7B1A. Classes of business

When a company decides that it wishes to transact insurance in the United Kingdom, lengthy forms have to be completed and submitted to the Department of Trade and Industry. One of the key items covered by these forms is the exact nature of the class of insurance which they wish to offer.

The 1974 Insurance Companies Act originally designated eight classes of business, in addition to ordinary and industrial life assurance. In 1977 the Insurance Companies (Classes of Business) Regulations came into effect and introduced into British legislation the seventeen classes used in the EEC Directive 73/239/EEC which we mentioned in 7A1G above. The 1982 Act maintains these classes and divides all insurance business in the United Kingdom into two groups, long term and general, with the various individual classes as follows:

Long Term
Class I	Life and Annuity
Class II	Marriage and Birth
Class III	Linked Long Term
Class IV	Permanent Health
Class V	Tontines
Class VI	Capital Redemption
Class VII	Pension Fund Management

General
Class 1	Accident
Class 2	Sickeness
Class 3	Land Vehicles
Class 4	Railway Rolling Stock
Class 5	Aircraft
Class 6	Ships
Class 7	Goods in Transit
Class 8	Fire and Natural Forces
Class 9	Damage to Property
Class 10	Motor Vehicle Liability

Class 11	Aircraft Liability
Class 12	Liability for Ships
Class 13	General Liability
Class 14	Credit
Class 15	Suretyship
Class 16	Miscellaneous Financial Loss
Class 17	Legal Expenses

It can be seen that these classes indicate forms of risk rather than forms of insurance business. For example, classes 10, 11, 12 and 13 are all different types of liability risk but are shown separately rather than as a type of insurance, i.e. liability insurance.

So that those who transact general business can identify which classes relate to which forms of business, the following schedule shows the old eight classes with which most people are familiar, and against each indicates which of the new classes apply.

Number	Designation	Composition
1	Accident and health	Classes 1 and 2
2	Motor	Classes 3, 7, 10 and part of class 1
3	Marine and transport	Classes 4, 6, 7, 12 and part of class 1
4	Aviation	Classes 5, 7, 11 and part of class 1
5	Fire and other damage to property	Classes 8 and 9
6	Liability	Classes 10, 11, 12 and 13
7	Credit and suretyship	Classes 14 and 15
8	General	All classes

Perhaps something should be about Class V of long term business. The 'Tontine' is now almost extinct as far as can be traced. It was a concept developed in the late seventeenth century and was a form of annuity. A group of people formed a 'Tontine' and would pay in a principal sum in return for an annuity for life. The difference between the Tontine and any ordinary annuity was that as members of the group died, their income from the Tontine was distributed among the survivors. The Tontine itself would end with the death of the last subscriber.

7B1B. Types of company seeking authorization

There are three basic forms of company described by the 1982 Act: UK Companies, Community Companies and External Companies. Separate authorization requirements apply to each type. We will look only at the general nature of the questioning of applicants rather than at the detail of any differences between the three basic forms of company. Firstly however let us distinguish, as the Act does, between the three types.

United Kingdom Companies. These are firms which have their head office in the UK and are formed under the Companies Act 1948 to 1981, or are registered societies or are established by Royal Charter or Act of Parliament.

Community Companies. A Community company is one which has its head office in one of the member states of the EEC, other than the UK, but nevertheless has a branch or some underwriting agency in the UK.

External Company. A company having its headquarters outside the EEC but having a branch or underwriting agency in the UK.

7B1C. Questions about authorization

The Secretary of State will not issue authorization to transact business unless, under the terms of 1982 Act, he is satisfied by all the information supplied to him by the applicant. This information is given on an application form, a different one being required for long term and general business; a different form is also required for UK, Community and External Companies.

The application forms are detailed and there would be little point in expecting readers to memorize the kind of information requested. In broad terms the forms ask for information concerning:

1. The company itself	including date of formation, objects, auditors, bankers, names of key personnel etc.
2. Scheme of operations	the source of business, premium tariffs, reinsurance arrangements, assets, costs of installing administrative services etc.,
3. Projections	Estimates over the first three financial years, of management expenses, premiums, claims, balance sheet etc.
4. Other information	Nature of investments, copies of reinsurance treaties, copies of agreements which the company will have with brokers or agents etc.

7B2.Solvency margins

The intention of a solvency margin and hence solvency margin regulations was stated in 7A1D when we looked at the 1946 Assurance Companies Act and the first introduction of margins of solvency. A relationship is established between assets and liabilities in such a way as to satisfy the regulatory body that the company is in a position to meet its liabilities. If the minimum solvency margin is not maintained then the Secretary of State has the power to intervene.

The regulations concerning solvency are contained in the Insurance Companies Act 1982 and the Insurance Company Regulations 1981. The actual value of the solvency margin, in monetary terms, varies from company to company. Obviously it would not be sensible to lay down one figure by which assets should exceed liabilities as there are vast differences in the volume of business transacted by insurance companies. What the Act does set out are certain formulae which produce given ratios. The actual formula depends upon the type of company i.e., UK, Community or External.

We will concentrate on UK companies, looking at the margins required for general business and long term business respectively.

First, it is necessary to note that, as a result of harmonization of solvency margins throughout the EEC, it is not possible for each member state to express its solvency margin regulations in terms of its own currency. This is a problem encountered in many other aspects of the Community's work and to overcome it the Community has created The European Currency Unit (ECU) which is a form of artificial currency to which all currencies of member states are fixed.

The ECU changes with movements in the currency of the member state itself and the conversion rate is fixed by the European Commission. For solvency margin purposes the conversion rate which is used in any year is the one fixed at the end of the preceding October. In other words, the ECU conversion rate for 1984 is the conversion rate fixed on the last day of October 1983. Conversion rates for the last four years have been:

1980	66.1903 p
1981	55.2376 p
1982	58.6509 p
1983	54.7783 p
1984	59.3782 p

7B2A.General business

The margin is determined by taking the greater of two sums resulting from the application of two sets of calculations called respectively First Method (premium basis) and Second Method (claims basis).

Premium basis
Gross premiums received are transferred into European Currency Units (ECU), at the current conversion rate. The company calculates 18% of the first 10 million ECU and 16% of any balance over and above 10 million. The resultant figure is then multiplied by 50% or a higher percentage if net claims paid (claims less reinsurance recoveries) is more than 50% of gross claims paid.

For example:

$$\text{Gross premiums} = 15\text{m ECU}$$

$$10\text{ m} \times 18\% = 1.8\text{m}$$
$$5\text{m} \times 16\% = \underline{0.8\text{m}}$$
$$2.6\text{m}$$

$$\text{Net claims paid} = 10\text{m}$$
$$\text{Gross claims paid} = 12\text{m}$$
$$= \frac{10}{12} \times 2.6\text{m} = 2.17\text{m ECU}$$

Claims basis
The total of all gross claims paid during the preceding three years is found, converted into ECU and the average taken. 26% is calculated of the first 7m ECU and 23% of any excess over 7m. The resultant figure is then multiplied by the same percentages as in the premium basis.

For example:

$$\text{Average claims paid 12m ECU}$$

$$7\text{m} \times 26\% = 1.82\text{m}$$
$$5\text{m} \times 23\% = \underline{1.15\text{m}}$$
$$2.97\text{m}$$

$$\text{Net claims paid} = 10\text{m}$$
$$\text{Gross claims paid} = 12\text{m}$$

$$= \frac{10}{12} \times 2.97\text{m} = 2.48\text{m ECU}$$

Guarantee funds

If a community company with its head office in the UK fails to maintain a margin of solvency at least equal to the greater of (*a*) the guarantee fund or (*b*) the minimum guarantee fund, the Secretary of State will ask the company to submit for his approval a short term financial scheme.

(*a*) *The guarantee fund* is one-third of the greater of the premium basis or the claims basis of calculating the margin of solvency.

(*b*) *The minimum guarantee funds* are shown below and are calculated according to the classes of business they write.

Class	Amount
10, 11, 12, 13, 14, 15	400,000 ECU
1, 2, 3, 4, 5, 6, 7, 8, 16	300,000 ECU
9, 17	200,000 ECU

In our example the claims basis produces the greater amount, namely 2.48m ECU. One-third of this is 826,667 ECU, which is the guarantee fund. This amount is greater than the minimum required to transact any class of business and it will become the solvency margin.

7B2B. Long term business

One major effect of implementing the EEC Life Establishment Directive, mentioned in 7A1G, has been the introduction of prescribed solvency margins for life assurers. These solvency margins applied to newly authorized companies from 1st January 1982 and to existing assurers from 15th March 1984.

The basic framework of solvency margins for life business is the same as that explained for general business. There is a ratio which is calculated and that must be maintained, subject to a minimum fund which varies according to the type of company i.e., Mutual Reinsurer or Proprietary.

The calculations are based, essentially, on actuarial liabilities and this is the main difference between life solvency and general solvency. In general business the solvency margin was determined by examining premiums and claims. In life business the claims are long-term and their actuarial value is calculated. In this way the life assurer is compelled to retain an adequate level of funds to meet these actuarially calculated liabilities.

A different set of calculations is required for Classes I & II, III & VII, IV & VI, and V. The required solvency margin for the company is then the aggregate of these different margins.

7B3. Monitoring

Having established a system of authorization of intending insurers and of determining solvency margins it is essential that there be some means by which the regulatory body can ensure that the standards are being maintained. Regular monitoring of companies is therefore an important aspect of the 1982 Act.

Each authorized insurer must prepare, and submit to the Department of Trade and Industry, a revenue account, profit and loss account and balance sheet in the prescribed manner. Life assurers must also appoint an actuary and submit a valuation of the long term fund once a year.

This continual monitoring of companies, while they are in the business of transacting insurance, should help in identifying those companies where trouble could be anticipated.

7B4. Intervention

The whole idea of monitoring the performance of companies will only be of value if the regulatory body can take some action if its monitoring highlights difficulties, Sections 37 to 46 of the 1982 Act set out the circumstances in which the Department of Trade and Industry may intervene and the powers which it can exercise. Clearly if a company fails to comply with any of the requirements laid down in the Act, such as the submission of accounts or the maintaining of solvency margins then the Department can and would intervene. In addition to these more obvious cases the Department can also intervene where, for example, the company has departed significantly from the business plan as set out in the original application, or a person has been appointed to a key position who is considered unsuitable to hold such a position.

In these and other cases, the Department has the power of intervention and can require the company, for example:

— to restrict its premium income;

— to submit accounts at more frequent intervals than a year;

— to supply any additional information over and above the accounts;

— to allow a full actuarial investigation of any life funds;

— to restrict the categories of investment which it makes.

These powers are far-reaching and could, effectively, bring a business to a standstill. They are not, however, used unwisely and it would only be in the case of a real likelihood of policyholders suffering that drastic action would be taken.

7B5.Conduct of business

The ten sections of Part III of the 1982 Act fall under the general heading of 'Conduct of Business'. These sections are concerned with the more day-to-day aspects of the company's business rather than with the broader financial aspects with which we have dealt so far.

The aspects of the business with which this part is concerned fall into a number of distinct areas including:

(i) *Advertisements*. Regulations concerning insurance advertisements are made in the Insurance Companies (Advertisements) (Amendment) (No. 2) Regulations 1983 SI 1983 No. 396. The chief aim of these regulations is to ensure that the public is adequately protected against possible misleading advertisements placed by life assurance companies not having head offices in the UK. Without going into too much detail we can say that the company placing the advertisement must state, if it is not an 'authorized insurer', that policyholders will not be protected by the Policyholders' Protection Act 1975.

(ii) *Misleading Statements*. This section of the Act makes it an offence to induce a person to effect insurance by *knowingly* making a misleading statement; for example, if a whole life contract with premiums ceasing at age 65 was knowingly misrepresented as a policy *maturing* at age 65.

(iii) *Connected Intermediaries*. Where an insurer has some connection with an intermediary, as in the case of an insurer which owns or has a controlling interest in a broker, this relationship must be disclosed to potential personal policyholders. This very much arose out of the Vehicle and General collapse where that company owned a broker, Andrew and Booth Ltd, and received a large volume of business from it. The current legislation would mean that that relationship would have to be revealed to clients of Andrew and Booth Ltd.

(iv) *'Cooling off' notices*. A potential policyholder of a long-term contract must be issued with a notice, in bold type, asking him to check that the policy meets his requirements. The notice is also to bring to his attention certain information relating to the payment of premiums, benefits, surrender values and paid-up policies. If the policyholder is not satisfied he can cancel the contract within a ten-day *cooling off* period without penalty.

7B6.Winding-up

In the end, if an insurance company has failed to meet the terms of the Act, it can be wound-up. This is the formal cessation of the life of the company and must be regarded as very much the final step after all other paths have been explored. This winding-up may be a voluntary act on the part of the company itself, compulsory by the Department of Trade or, interestingly, by ten or more policyholders who have policies with an aggregate value of not less than £10,000.

7C.Why have State regulation?

Having looked at both the development and current status of governmental intervention in insurance activities we can suggest some reasons why such supervision is necessary. The words control, regulation, supervision and intervention are being looked upon as interchangeable, although some have attached separate meanings to each. For our purposes we can say that governments have taken more than a passing interest in the transaction of insurance and whether we say this interest amounted to intervention, control, regulation or supervision is incidental to the question, 'why have State regulation?' The main justification for State control is to protect the public but this aim is also accompanied by one relating to socially desirable measures. In the following list items (*a*) to (*c*) relate to protection and (*d*) to (*f*) to social measures:

(*a*) *Maintain solvency*. Perhaps the greatest step taken by legislation was to introduce solvency margins that were related to premium income. In this way a ratio was established between the margin and the amount of business undertaken. This prevented certain people, with fraudulent aims, from providing insurance and acted as a continual monitor on those already transacting it.

(*b*) *Equity*. The term equity has been used but equally suitable would have been morality, fairness or reasonableness, as each implies the fact that an element of fairness must exist between companies and policyholder. The insurance contract is one of considerable complexity and it is essential that controls exist for the protection of policyholders.

(*c*) *Competence*. The buying and selling of insurance is unlike many other forms of product purchasing. A tangible product is not being purchased; a promise to provide indemnity, an exact compensation, is what is being bought and sold. It is necessary that those who deal in such promises are competent persons and able to fulfil their pledges when the need arises. Regulations are necessary therefore in the management of insurance companies.

(*d*) *Insurable interest*. Insurable interest is one of the basic doctrines of insurance. Governments have found it necessary to introduce legislation to eradicate any element of gambling. It was not acceptable that unscrupulous persons should benefit by effecting policies of insurances where they had no financial interest in the potential loss other than the profit they would make if it occurred.

(*e*) *Provision of certain forms of insurance.* An element of intervention has been in evidence where forms of cover have been made compulsory, as in the case of employers' liability and third party motor accident injuries. The intervention is not in the provision of cover by government, but in establishing the nature of the cover to be granted.

(*f*) *National Insurance.* For some areas of social risk the government's intervention has been total and it has assumed the responsibility for providing certain covers. A full examination of National Insurance schemes is undertaken in chapter 9 and it is sufficient to say here that for areas such as unemployment, sickness and widows' benefits the State carries the risk under the National scheme.

7D. Insurance Brokers (Registration) Act 1977

Until recently anyone could describe themselves as an insurance broker whether they had any insurance knowledge or not, and it was difficult for the public to distinguish the genuine professional expert from the amateur. At least 9000 firms called themselves brokers (compared with many tens of thousands of part-time agents) and there were four organisations of brokers which sought to maintain varying standards of conduct for their members. These organisations were Lloyd's Insurance Brokers' Association (LIBA), the Corporation of Insurance Brokers (CIB), the Association of Insurance Brokers (AIB) and the Federation of Insurance Brokers (FIB). It was felt desirable within the insurance broking industry that there should be one body to represent the profession and to supervise the standing and operations of those permitted to call themselves insurance brokers.

In January 1976, the four associations established the British Insurance Brokers' Council (BIBC) which prepared proposals with the approval of the Secretary of State for Trade for the registration and regulation of insurance brokers. It proposed the creation of a Registration Council which would satisfy itself as to the experience, qualifications and financial status of applicants for registration as brokers. The proposals of the Brokers' Council were the basis of a Private Member's Bill which became The Insurance Brokers (Registration) Act on 29 July 1977.

Having achieved its purpose, the British Insurance Brokers' Council was disbanded in 1977 along with the four independent associations and the British Insurance Brokers' Association (BIBA) was formed.

Under the 1977 Act, the Insurance Brokers' Registration Council (IBRC) was established to govern the registration and regulation of insurance brokers. The IBRC is a legally created separate independent body from the BIBA which is a voluntary trade association.

7D1. Insurance Brokers' Registration Council

The Act did not become fully operative on receiving the Royal Assent, but will come into force over a period of time. Initially, the Council comprises 17 members, 12 of whom are nominated by BIBA but once fully implemented these members will be nominated by the registered brokers, and the remaining 5 members are government nominees.

The register was opened for applications at the end of 1978 and it is the Council's remit to draw up a code of conduct for registered members, establish a complaints investigating committee, and a disciplinary committee with powers to 'strike off' members whose breach of regulations warrants such action.

From 1 December 1981 it has been illegal for anyone to describe himself as an insurance broker if he is not registered under the Act. This, however, does not prevent anyone calling himself an insurance adviser or consultant, nor the part-time agents continuing as before.

7D1A. Registration of individuals

For an individual to be registered he must:

(*a*) hold an approved qualification*; or

(*b*) have carried on business as, or have been employed by, an insurance broker or full-time agent for at least two companies, or been employed by an insurance company, for at least five years; or

(*c*) hold a recognized qualification* and have carried on business, or been employed as in (*b*) above, for at least three years.

(*At present the only qualifications recognized for the purposes of registration are the Associateship or Fellowship of the Chartered Insurance Institute, but the Council has power to accept others.)

The individual must satisfy the Council that he has had suitable work experience.

Sole traders, partnerships and limited companies must comply with further conditions regarding solvency, accounting practices and professional indemnity insurance cover. In the case of limited companies, at least half the directors must be registered insurance brokers and the code of conduct requires that all work shall be under the day-to-day supervision of registered persons.

Readers should keep abreast of the developing legislation in this area, as new requirements can be implemented under the 1977 Act by statutory instruments from time to time.

7E. Compulsory insurance

We said earlier that one form which government supervision had taken was the passing of legislation making certain forms of insurance compulsory; the following are in that category.

7E1. Motor insurance

The Road Traffic Act 1972, part VI, consolidates previous legislation. Section 143 of the Act states, 'Subject to the provisions of this part of this Act, it shall not be lawful for a person to use, or cause or permit another person to use, a motor vehicle on a road unless there is in force in relation to the use of the vehicle by that person or that other person, as the case may be, such a policy of insurance or such a security in respect of third party risks as complies with the requirement of this Part of this Act . . .'

In brief we can say that:

(*a*) The third party risks referred to are death of or bodily injury to any person. This will include pedestrians, passengers in other cars, passengers in the policy-holder's car and any other person at all.

(*b*) The security, in place of insurance, is a deposit of £15,000 with the Accountant General of the Supreme Court and this will remove the need to insure only when the car is driven under the control of the insured.

(*c*) A certificate of insurance is to be issued and a policy will not be effective in the terms of the Road Traffic Act unless one is. Note that a certificate of insurance is one of the documents required before a person can obtain a road fund licence.

(*d*) It is the user of the car, not the driver, who must be covered by insurance and a person will be deemed to have the use of a car when he retains an element of control, management or operation of the vehicle at the relevant time.

(*e*) The policy of insurance is to be issued by an 'authorised' insurer, that is, an insurer carrying on motor insurance in Great Britain and who has satisfied the requirement of the Insurance Companies Act 1974. Such an insurer must also be a member of the Motor Insurers' Bureau.

7E2. Employers' liability insurance

The Employers' Liability (Compulsory Insurance) Act 1969 came into effect on 1 January 1972 and from that date every employer carrying on business in Scotland, England and Wales has to insure against liability for bodily injury or disease sustained by employees and arising from their employment. Note the following points (separate statutes apply to other parts of the UK):

(*a*) The Act only refers to bodily injury and disease and while it therefore covers a whole range of problems it does not include any element of property damage.

(*b*) The policy must be effected with an 'authorised' insurer and in this connection the points applying above regarding an 'authorised' motor insurer apply here also.

(*c*) A certificate of insurance is to be issued and must be displayed at every place of business.

(*d*) The person injured must be employed by the policyholder and the injury or disease must arise out of that employment.

(*e*) Certain employers need not insure, such as local government councils and industries under national ownership or control.

7E3. Riding establishments

By the Riding Establishments Act of 1970, which amended the Riding Establishments Act of 1964, any person who holds a licence to run a riding establishment must have certain liability insurance. Insurance is to be held against liability for any injury sustained by a person who hires a horse or who is being instructed and is also required for liability which may be incurred by the hirer in connection with injury caused to any other person. As an interesting aside, the Act refers to horses as including any, 'mare, gelding, pony, foal, colt, filly or stallion and also any ass, mule or jennet'. As might be expected, the incidence of jennets causing injury is rare and the law reports have little reference to cases under the Act.

7E4. Nuclear risks

The organisations holding a licence to operate a nuclear plant, in this country usually government agencies, have a duty imposed upon them by the Nuclear Installations Act 1965 to ensure that no injury or damage is caused either on or off the site by nuclear perils. A further stipulation is that funds are to be made available to meet any liabilities devolving upon the operator by way of insurance or other approved means. The amount to be made available is £5m for each nuclear installation and is an aggregate amount, that is, it will reduce with each claim payment. This £5m is not the limit of funding against the nuclear peril as the Government has made provision for compensation up to £43m per occurrence.

7E5. Solicitors' professional indemnity

By the Solicitors' Act 1974 it is now compulsory for every solicitor to carry professional indemnity insurance with a limit of indemnity amounting to at least £50,000, or £30,000 for each partner in a partnership.

7E6. Oil pollution

One problem of comparatively recent origin is the damage done by oil spillage from merchant ships. There have been several examples of this recently resulting in substantial damage to fish stocks, bird life and coast lines. The Merchant Shipping (Oil Pollution) Act 1971, as amended by the Merchant Shipping Act 1974, states that certain oil carrying vessels must have a certificate of insurance before they can enter or leave a port or terminal.

7E7. Why have compulsory insurance?

There are one or two additional areas where insurance is required, but is not compulsory, such as in the case of contractors who want a tax exemption certificate from the Inland Revenue having to hold public liability insurance, and mortgagors buying a house and the building society insisting on buildings insurance. These are not strictly speaking compulsory. Why, then, are certain forms of insurance compulsory in particular cases? The following are suggested as being among the reasons:

(a) *The provision of funds.* There would be no point in awarding damages to someone if there were no money to meet the award. Notice that the insurance is for liability against injury, except in the case of nuclear sites when damage is also included, thus emphasizing the importance placed upon injury in the eyes of the law. The enactment of compulsory insurance ensures, as far as possible, that funds will be available when damages are awarded. An interesting point for discussion is the extent to which this fact influences the eventual size of the award, if in fact it influences it at all.

(b) *Eases the State's burden.* It is unlikely that the State would allow people injured at work, or in similar accidents to go without compensation entirely and if the responsible party did not have funds to provide this the likelihood is that the State would come forward with some money. The existence of insurance eliminates this possibility.

(c) *The response to national concern.* Apart from riding establishments, the areas where insurance has been made compulsory represent areas of national concern. When we traced the development of motor and employers' liability insurance we saw how public attitudes changed over the years until concern over accidents was so high that legislation was introduced to ensure the provision of insurance. Nuclear risks is a far more recent area of concern and it may be pertinent to note that it is the only risk where insurance is required for injury or damage. This may be due partly to the grave concern voiced by many and to the difficulties that could be involved in trying to separate injury and damage claims when radioactive material leaked from some installation.

(d) *Protection.* It is not suggested that by making a person insure you also make him more careful, thus assisting in the protection of the potential injured persons. This may or may not be true, but what can be said with more certainty is that as insurance is involved the insured will be exposed to all the expertise available from insurers and the exercising of this expertise may improve the risk and thus assist in protecting people. An example from the employers' liability field could be the case where a liability surveyor from an insurance company insists on special guards on machines to minimise the risk of injury. The insured may not have contemplated doing this himself but is forced to by the insurers.

7F. Nationalisation

The ultimate step in Government supervision would be complete nationalisation.

In 1976 the Labour Party accepted proposals, at its annual conference, for nationalisation of Britain's seven largest insurance companies and in 1978 the insurance industry completed its evidence to the Wilson Committee that had been set up to review the functioning of insurance institutions. As yet no companies have been nationalised but this does not mean that the issue is dead and we should certainly acquaint ourselves with the arguments for and against. The topic is one that arouses deep feelings with certain people and it is often difficult to put forward a balanced objective portrayal of the pros and cons. The following represent certain of the basic points on each side.

7F1. For nationalisation

(a) Governmental control of funds would be to the benefit of society at large.
(b) It would be possible to introduce uniformity in wordings and practice.
(c) Statistics could be pooled.
(d) Premium rates could be reduced in the absence of the profit motive.

(*e*) The costly exercise of making the statutory returns would be eliminated.

(*f*) There would not be so great a reliance on reinsurance with a commensurate saving in costs.

(*g*) It may be better if those forms of insurance made compulsory by government were provided by the State.

7F2. Against nationalisation

(*a*) It is difficult to 'nationalise the international'. It could be that some overseas countries would not trade with a government-owned insurance industry.

(*b*) Insurance has grown and developed in private hands for many centuries and there is no reason to think that any better service would result from State ownership.

(*c*) Experience of certain nationalised industries is one of overloaded bureaucracy.

(*d*) Competition encourages efficiency and innovation.

(*e*) The present tax revenue from insurance companies would be lost.

(*f*) The large scale nature of any State insurance organisation may lead to a strictness in practice and interpretation that would not benefit the public.

(*g*) The government has no experience in underwriting insurable risks.

8. The international role of insurance

8A.Historical development

Since the start of international trading the need for insurance cover has related to risks external to national boundaries, although initially the insured was based in the country of origin of the venture and any cover required was arranged there. The risks to be insured related to goods and their means of transport.

As trade developed, the trading nations established agencies and branches in foreign countries, and brought to these countries the customs of trade and commerce including insurance.

The London insurance market, although by no means the largest in premium income, is, however, the leading market of the world, and at this point it is appropriate to examine the reasons for its growth and importance.

8A1.Reasons for international development

During the 17th, 18th, 19th and early part of the 20th centuries Britain was a great trading nation, and various explorers and merchants opened up hitherto undiscovered countries. We saw in chapter 3 how these maritime ventures led to the establishment of Lloyd's. This was paralleled with the growth of insurance companies to cope with increasing losses, mainly through fire, in Britain. The expansion of marine insurance and other classes (see chapter 3) were complementary to each other, in that when trading companies established premises abroad they insured them in the same market which was used for their UK risks – London.

As nationals of the developing countries established businesses it was natural, in the first instance, for them to follow the lead of the early settlers and seek insurance in the London market.

International trade required other help by way of finance and banking facilities, so that London developed as the leading centre for these facilities also.

The provision by Lloyd's of international news and information services was of considerable advantage to the traders and they were expanded as a deliberate aid to their international insurance trade (Sir Henry Mance, 1973).

We shall look later at the style or form which the development took, but the branch offices and subsidiary companies established abroad by British insurers gave this country a unique knowledge and expertise of insurance requirements and operations worldwide.

London had become a strong and developed centre for trade, banking, finance, and insurance by 1800, and it was in the 19th century that the greatest expansion of international insurance took place. Before looking at this development, let us consider the advantages and disadvantages of an international insurance facility.

London still survives as the leading world centre for insurance, in security, prestige and expertise if not in volume. One of the reasons for this is the manner in which British insurers met their liabilities abroad at the height of world expansion in insurance business when local companies failed. The Hamburg fire of 1842, the Chicago fire of 1869 and the San Francisco earthquake of 1906 saw the London market meeting its losses, while sectors of the German and American markets failed in the wake of these catastrophes. The reputation and security, established at that time and maintained since, have sustained our position as world leaders.

8A1A.Advantages of international development

(*a*) the basic concept of insurance is that by spreading risk, the effect of loss will be carried by the insuring public as a whole rather than the one individual who has the loss. We have seen in chapter 5 that this principle can be extended from the private individual to the insurance company by way of reinsurance. By extension, it is desirable that the risks of one country be shared by others, particularly where some of the risks may be of a catastrophic nature when viewed from the capacity of one country's insurance market. The possibility of a Thames flood in London, or another earthquake in San Francisco are topical examples of such catastrophes;

(b) the underwriting results of particular classes of insurance, and indeed of particular countries, tend to operate in cycles of heavy losses and reasonable profits. There is usually a time lag in the response to deteriorating claims experience by way of stricter underwriting or higher premiums, so that from a purely national viewpoint, the fluctuations in profit levels can be very severe, making financial management more difficult. Viewed internationally there are usually favourable results in some markets at the same time as disastrous ones in others. An international spread of risk by the leading insurers in each country will help to even out the peaks and troughs, thus leading to more stable markets. This is to the long term benefit of policyholders everywhere;

(c) in any developed country there are likely to be multinational commercial organisations requiring cover on a worldwide basis. If the insurance market of the parent company is to retain as much of the premium income of that parent as possible, it is essential that staff are experienced in the risks of foreign countries and are aware of the pertaining insurance regulations. There is no better way to achieve the expertise required than to participate actively in as many countries as possible and with as wide a portfolio as possible;

(d) where a nation has a large amount of foreign trade, it is desirable that its financial services are developed in parallel, not only to facilitate that trade, but as freestanding currency earners in their own right. We have seen how the London insurance market grew in this way and the major contribution which it makes to 'invisible exports' (figure 2/1). We now see that as Japan has developed as a major trading nation, it too has become a major provider of international insurance cover.

8A1B. Disadvantages of international development

(a) insurance companies which have been established overseas for many years are finding that the legislation being introduced is rapidly making it more and more difficult to continue operating with the same volume of business. The developing countries, in particular, are becoming more and more nationalistic in their outlook on insurance activity. Aggressive marketing by local and other foreign companies is reducing Britain's share of many markets. For prestige purposes it may be desirable to retain a presence, but at a cost to profits;

(b) in certain countries there is active political prejudice against foreign companies and the rates of premium they can charge;

(c) the same economies of scale in operating costs are not possible as at home, or as available to the national companies in the country of operation. The result is that the foreign company is less competitive;

(d) international development by British companies leads to the establishment of strong home based insurers in the overseas countries. They in turn tend to expand their interests to Britain. This can have a significant effect, if overseas practices and methods of reinsurance are used here, as can be seen from the American influence on the British fire insurance market in recent years.

8A2. Nature of foreign development

British insurers have clearly felt that the advantages of foreign development outweighed the disadvantages as over many years they have gradually expanded the extent of their foreign involvement.

The way in which this development took place is dealt with in a book by H. E. Raynes, 'A History of British Insurance', but here we can broadly identify four main ways.

8A2A. Home foreign departments

Home foreign departments are the head office departments of British companies, which have been established to underwrite foreign business. Where an insured or proposer has risks outside of Britain it would be this department which would consider that aspect of the overall portfolio.

This method of transacting foreign business obviates the need for, and expense of operating, a network of branches or agents overseas. Ultimately, however, some local expertise will be required if only to survey risks.

8A2B. Overseas agencies

Another method of transacting overseas busines, this time not relying on all enquiries and decisions being centralized at the UK head office, is to create a number of overseas agents. These agents could be local business or professional people who have been given authority, subject to certain limits, to issue policies and settle claims.

This system also helps to reduce the cost of establishing an overseas operation but, as with everything, there is a cost. The price the company presumably is prepared to pay is that its own qualified insurance personnel are not handling the business since authority has been handed over to an agent.

8A2C. Overseas branches

As the volume of business increases it will become less easy to handle it all through an agent, even a very efficient agent. Eventually a representation will be required in the country concerned and this will inevitably mean a branch office. Clearly the scale of this branch operation depends upon the volume of business written in the country but there will be a point at which the branch becomes a more attractive alternative to either the overseas agent or the home foreign department.

Once established, the branch can become a much more effective marketing tool than either of the other two methods. There may, however, be areas in the world where restrictive legislation may not allow branches of foreign companies to operate; we shall look briefly at this later.

8A2D. Subsidiary and associated companies

One way to overcome restrictive legislation is to either acquire a controlling interest in a local company or come to some trading arrangement with a local company.

If a controlling interest can be obtained in a company which is permitted to transact business in the foreign country in which you are interested then this would be a reasonable way for you to conduct your foreign business. The local company would have its own share of the market and have local expertise.

The same advantages are to be gained if it is possible for you to come to some trading arrangement with a foreign company whereby they agree to service your business in their country and you agree to service their business in your country.

8A3. Restrictions on international development

The main restriction to a company setting up operations in a foreign country is that there is often some form of State control on the establishment of foreign insurance companies. British insurers have not been nearly so successful in entering the European markets as they have others. The reasons for this are the much tighter State control which exists in European countries, the political and national changes which took place in Europe up to 1945, and keen local competition.

State control may well be desirable and on a national basis within Europe, T. H. Ellis (1980) suggests that this is to protect policyholders, third party claimants, shareholders and the survival of the company. These ideas apply elsewhere in the world also. So far as foreign insurers are concerned, the controls on reserves and operations may make it impossible or impracticable for a foreign company to wish to operate. An increasing number of countries are going further and passing legislation which prohibits the placing of insurance with companies not licensed locally. The licensing regulations may prohibit overseas companies from applying.

These latter restrictions are designed to protect and further the well-being of local insurers. It is most evident in the former British colonies which are rapidly developing and wish to develop a healthy insurance industry to support their domestic and foreign trade.

Prior to the creation of the European Economic Community (the EEC) and the effective dates of various directives, such restrictions were also common in West Germany, France and Italy. Other countries have gone even further and nationalised their insurance industry.

While such restrictions enable local insurers to expand to the detriment of outsiders, they have some inherent dangers for the countries involved. We mentioned that international insurance operations were one method of spreading the risk to a country's national insurance market of a national disaster, or destruction of a major plant producing a country's main product. Such losses could place new national insurers, which have not yet fully developed, in serious financial difficulties.

Some countries have recognised this fact and allow international placings of reinsurance business while still restricting direct operations to local companies.

Even where foreign insurers are allowed to operate either directly or through reinsurance, there may be foreign exchange restrictions on the amount of the repatriation of funds and profits allowable per annum.

8B. Importance of overseas markets

The existence of overseas markets implies an in-flow of premiums to the United Kingdom. Let us first of all establish the size of the flow of premiums and then try to gauge its importance to the economy.

8B1. Volume of foreign business

It would be an almost impossible task to obtain premium figures from all insurers transacting business and it is just as difficult to obtain premium figures from UK insurers. Fortunately, however, the British Insurance Association gathers excellent statistical information from its approximately 340 member companies. These companies transact about 95% of the worldwide business of the British market. By looking at their statistics over the past five years we can build some picture of the volume of foreign business. Figure 8/1 illustrates Net Premium Income.

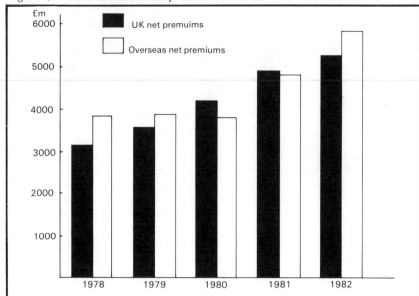

Figure 8/1. General business net premium income UK and overseas 1978–82

Source: BIA Facts and Figures

There is no determinable trend in the volume of overseas business written by British insurers, but two points are noticeable. Firstly, the UK net premium income has steadily grown and secondly the volume of overseas net written premiums is very close to the UK figure.

To these figures for BIA companies must be added Lloyd's premium income which for the period 1978–1982 was as follows:

Lloyd's worldwide premiums.

	£m
1978	2052
1979	2245
1980	2595
1981	3942
1982	2504

Source: BIA Statistics Bureau.

These figures represent the total premiums received in these calendar years. In 1982 approximately 29% of the total premium income of Lloyd's was made up of UK business. In other words approximately £1778m was derived from overseas business.

Adding this figure to the £5836m generated from overseas by BIA companies gives a total figure of £7614m of premiums relating to overseas business.

8B2. Importance to economy

These figures on premium income do not however show what the country *earns* from attracting overseas business. From the total premiums written must be deducted claims and expenses, and finally any overseas investment income must be added. These overseas earnings are shown in figure 8/2 for the period 1978–1982.

Figure 8/2. Overseas earnings of the Insurance Industry, 1978–1982 (in £m)

	1978	1979	1980	1981	1982
Underwriting					
–companies	313	278	186	150	102
–Lloyd's	354	312	188	254	215
	667	590	374	404	317
–less earnings of UK branches					
of overseas companies	13	16	28	29	29
	654	574	346	375	288
Overseas Portfolio					
investment income	148	207	264	299	524
UK brokers' overseas					
earnings	237	228	238	302	362
	1039	1009	848	976	1174

Source: UK Balance of Payments (HMSO)

These figures on their own do not illustrate the importance of overseas insurance earnings. To measure that, we will have to compare these earnings with other earnings and this comparison may be made in two stages. Firstly, we can compare the insurance earnings with those of other financial services and secondly we can look at these total financial services in relation to the overall Balance of Payments.

Figure 8/3 shows our first comparison.

Figure 8/3. Net Invisible Earnings 1978–1982 £m

	1978	1979	1980	1981	1982
Insurance	1039	1009	848	976	1174
Banking	701	212	457	1340	1656
Commodity trading	295	285	340	360	449
Brokerage	248	331	370	490	481
Other	135	182	277	348	609
TOTAL	2418	2019	2292	3514	4369

Source: BIA Facts & Figures

These financial service earnings are referred to as 'invisible' earnings which we have already discussed in chapter 2. From figure 8/3 it can be seen that insurance represents a significant proportion of all invisible earnings. On average, over the five years shown in the table, insurance has accounted for more than a third of the total invisible earnings of the country.

The overall balance of payments position for the five years 1978–1982 is shown in figure 8/4.

Figure 8/4. UK Balance of Payments 1978–1982 (£m)

	1978	1979	1980	1981	1982
Net trade (the difference between visible exports and imports)	−1542	−3449	1233	3008	2119
Invisible earnings	2418	2019	2292	3514	4369

Source: UK Balance of Payments (HMSO)

It can be seen here that the balance of trade took a sharp up-turn in 1980. This was due to the increasing revenue from the export of North Sea Oil, a phenomenon which some believe will be short-lived. However, even when oil exports are included in the figures, the amount earned by invisibles, of which we have seen that insurance represents about a third, is still greater.

We shall now look at the geographical division of Britain's overseas premium earnings and then concentrate on two of our most important markets.

8B3.The source of overseas business

It is extremely difficult to obtain figures which show the geographical split of premium income. However Carter and Godden in their book *The British Insurance Industry: A Statistical Review* give information extracted from the published accounts of eleven major British insurers showing the source of their overseas business. These eleven companies, for 1982, represent 79% of the total volume of general overseas business as shown in figure 8/1 for all BIA member companies and hence form a useful base upon which to draw certain conclusions. Figure 8/5 illustrates the source of overseas business over the last five years.

Figure 8/5. Source of overseas business 1978–82 (£m)

	1978	1979	1980	1981	1982
United States	1305 (42%)	1288 (42%)	1304 (44%)	1836 (48%)	2345 (51%)
Canada	464 (15%)	443 (14%)	431 (14%)	579 (15%)	653 (14%)
Australia	219 (7%)	198 (6%)	183 (6%)	210 (5%)	257 (6%)
Europe	654 (21%)	655 (21%)	585 (20%)	634 (17%)	695 (15%)
Others	496 (15%)	488 (17%)	482 (16%)	580 (15%)	651 (14%)
TOTAL	3138 (100%)	3072 (100%)	2985 (100%)	3839 (100%)	4601 (100%)

The figures in the brackets show the percentage of the premium income derived from the various areas. Figure 8/6 shows the same figures but illustrates them in a slightly different way.

It can be seen from this diagram that the United States market is by far the largest source of overseas business. In 1982 it amounted to over half of all overseas business written by those eleven companies mentioned earlier. Europe comes next and when Europe is added to the United States market then we can see that about two thirds of overseas business is generated from America and Europe.

This highlights the importance of the United States and European markets and it is upon these two we will now concentrate.

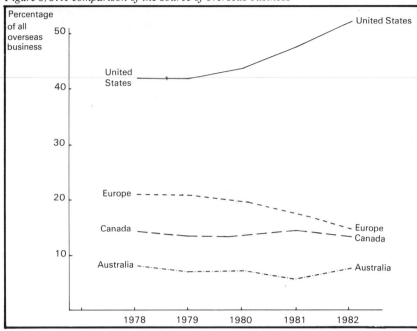

Figure 8/6. A comparison of the source of overseas business

8C. The United States markets

Clearly, the United States market is extremely important, both in terms of the share of the world market which it retains and the volume of business written there by UK companies.

The United States is by far the largest single market for insurance in the world. It is difficult to say exactly what proportion of all business is accounted for by the United States but an approximation of 50% is realistic.

Given the gigantic volume of business underwritten in the United States then it is clear that the British market must be heavily involved in it. While a substantial proportion of all overseas business written by British companies is derived from the United States, this is not in itself a measure of how important the market is. To ascertain this we could look at the profit derived from the business written. If we look for example at Fire & Accident and Motor results in the United States we have the figures in figure 8/7.

Figure 8/7. United States Underwriting Results — 1978–1982

	1978	1979	1980	1981	1982
Fire and Accident	2.3	−0.6	−2.7	−6.0	−15.5
	(0.2)	(−1.9)	(−0.3)	(−1.5)	(−10.2)
Motor	0.3	−3.7	−7.4	−11.8	−17.1
	(−2.0)	(−4.2)	(−3.8)	(−0.5)	(−4.5)

Source: BIA Facts & Figures

The figures in figure 8/7 represent the profit or loss expressed as a percentage of premium income and so in the case of Fire & Accident business in 1982 there was a loss amounting to 15.5% of the premium income. The figures in brackets are those for UK business only and it can be seen that the American experience has steadily deteriorated.

8C1. United States trends

We have said that the US accounts for about 50% of worldwide business. This share has reduced from the high figure of 62% in 1965. This reduction in the US market mirrors the growth in other markets but it still points to the very important rôle which the US plays. (Over the same period since 1965 the Japanese market, for example, has increased by a factor of over three).

Over this time also, if we look at the internal US market, we find that UK companies have lost substantial ground. Given what we have said about poor underwriting results, which in themselves may cause British companies to withdraw, we could cite a number of additional reasons why this ground may have been lost:

(*a*) The fierce competition from direct selling by US companies. This phenomenon is now prominent in the UK life scene. British companies may have been slow to respond to this form of marketing.

(*b*) In the 1960's several British insurers withdrew from many of the States because of alleged protection to home based insurers by the State Insurance Commissioners. Even where these companies have returned they may well have lost ground permanently.

(c) Agents have the legal right to renew contracts and can switch business to obtain higher commission rates.

(d) US Mutuals have an excellent record for service and claims service and not only the British companies but many US proprietary companies also have lost ground to them.

(e) There has been a growth in risk management risk financing techniques and it is possible that American companies have been more willing to accommodate the requests of large buyers of insurance than have British companies.

Before leaving the US market it is worthwhile pointing out that over the late seventies and early eighties links between British and US insurance brokers strengthened. The following table shows some of the better known connections.

1978	Leslie & Godwin acquired by Frank B. Hall
1980	C. T. Bowring acquired by Marsh & McLennan
1980	Wigham Poland 57% acquired by Fred S. James
1981	Alexander Howden acquired by Alexander & Alexander.

Here we can see that four of the US's major brokers now have transatlantic links. These links are all with Lloyd's brokers, thus giving the American broker direct access to the important market place of Lloyd's.

8D. The European market

We saw in figures 8/5 and 8/6 that Europe was a significant source of overseas business. The European share of world premiums is also significant, standing at about 25%. However, the British share of this Western European market has declined. This decline could be attributable to a number of causes but in the main it would have to be said that there has been a more rapid increase in productivity on the continent of Europe than in Britain. This could then account for the increased volume of business generated on the continent. Linked with this is the fact that the range of covers offered on the continent was narrower than in Britain for many years, but now this imbalance has been redressed.

8E. Other overseas markets

The rest of the world is a very important market for British interests, earning for us over 34% of our total world non-life income in 1982. This income comes from the greater proportion of countries. For example, one leading British insurer operates directly or through associates in 78 different territories, and most of the leading companies will have a similar spread of risk. In total they operate in over 100 countries. This wide spread, as has been mentioned earlier, helps to generate new business from many diverse areas and in the long run leads to some stability in the worldwide underwriting results of the companies which can vary substantially from year to year in particular countries. In many cases, but by no means all, the commonwealth and ex-colonial countries are involved in this spread. Their preference for the London market is understandable since historically they are familiar with British terms and practice.

Within the developing countries there may be a tendency to increased nationalism or nationalisation, to the restriction or exclusion of overseas insurers. Many of these countries have serious balance of payments and foreign exchange problems, and so one can see the logic in trying to build up their domestic insurance market. In many cases there is a strong affinity to British insurance, and The Chartered Insurance Institute and various colleges in the UK provide valuable education and training for their trainee executives. Several UK companies are actively helping local insurers to set up their national organisations. All of these points may contribute to the replacement of former direct business with reinsurance business in London instead of elsewhere.

8F. Conclusion

In some areas of the world the influence of British insurance may be diminishing slightly. The USA, Japan and West Germany have larger shares of world premium income than the UK, but none can compare with London for prestige, expertise and know-how, and many overseas countries will wish to see their risks insured in the pound sterling in London.

References
Sir Henry Mance, *'Lloyd's' and the International Scene*, CII Journal No. 70 1973
H. E. Raynes, *A History of British Insurance*, Pitman 1968
T. H. Ellis, *European Integration & Insurance*, Witherby 1980
R. L. Carter and A. H. Godden, *Statistical Review*, Klower & Harrap 1983.

9. National insurance and social security

9A.Historical development

National Insurance is really outside the scope of activities of those engaged in commercial insurance but a knowledge of what is involved in the National scheme is important, not only for the purposes of examination, but also for the sake of completing and rounding off our knowledge of insurance protection.

9A1.Background

Almost all who will read this book will have spent their entire lives under the protection of some form of Welfare State. In these circumstances it is extremely difficult for us to cast our minds back to pre-welfare state days but such days did exist and harsh they were.

Many plays, books and films portray the lot of those unfortunates who found themselves unable to earn a living through ill health or just through lack of jobs. The Elizabethan Poor Law Act 1601 really marked the start of the State assuming some responsibility for social security and the relief of poverty was placed on the parish within which a person lived.

The eighteenth and nineteenth centuries saw the progression of poor laws and the existence of workhouses, and with the Industrial Revolution and the move towards towns the position was acute. Some employers did a little to help employees but the position was bleak, well described in many Dickens novels, especially for the underprivileged such as orphans, widows and the elderly.

9A2.State intervention

A Royal Commission on poor law and relief was established in 1905 and it recommended the separate treatment of sickness, unemployment and old age. A National Insurance Act was passed in 1911 introducing the three-fold method of payment involving employers, employees and the State. The Act provided for sickness and maternity benefits for manual and certain non-manual workers. The Act also introduced unemployment insurance. A number of amending statutes were passed in following years but the landmark came in 1942 with the publication of the Beveridge Report on Social Insurance and Allied Services. The government accepted the report in principle and an extended scheme of National Insurance began in August 1948.

9B.National Insurance and Social Security today

Britain's current system dates back to the 1940s and the Beveridge Report. There are around 60 different cash benefits available to help people in times of need. The extensive nature of the system does lead to confusion and complications. Knowing how much they are entitled to and how to claim benefits is often a problem for many people, particularly when they are suffering from some hardship which the benefit is intended to alleviate.

The Department of Health and Social Security under whose province the National Insurance and Social Security system falls, does, however, produce a wide range of leaflets. These leaflets (see figure 9/1 for some examples) are freely available from local DHSS offices and are supplemented regularly by advertisements in the media pointing out the availability of certain benefits. Despite these efforts it is estimated that, at any one time, a significant amount of money in benefits is not taken up by people who are entitled to them.

9B1.Type of benefits

No advantage exists in trying to draw hard and fast lines between national insurance and social security. Any lines so drawn often tend later to be shown as inaccurate, due to exceptions from common principles. It is easier to look at the benefits themselves and categorise them. There are three main types.

9B1A.National Insurance benefits

These benefits can be claimed if a person, or on some occasions the spouse, has paid a sufficient number of National Insurance contributions. More on the question of contributions follows.

Unemployment benefit is an example of a National Insurance benefit. A person who normally works, is fit and available for work, but is out of work qualifies for this benefit. The unemployed person registers at the local employment office or job centre and draws unemployment benefit. The retirement pension, death grant, maternity allowance and widow's allowance are further examples of national insurance benefits.

9B1B.Non-contributory benefits

These benefits depend only on whether a person seeking them meets certain conditions. No National Insurance contributions are needed and there is no means test, that is, no

Figure 9/1. National insurance leafl

Which benefit?
cash help
National insurance contribution rates
From 6 April 1980
security
efit rat
om Novemb
Catalogue of
social security leaflets
60+

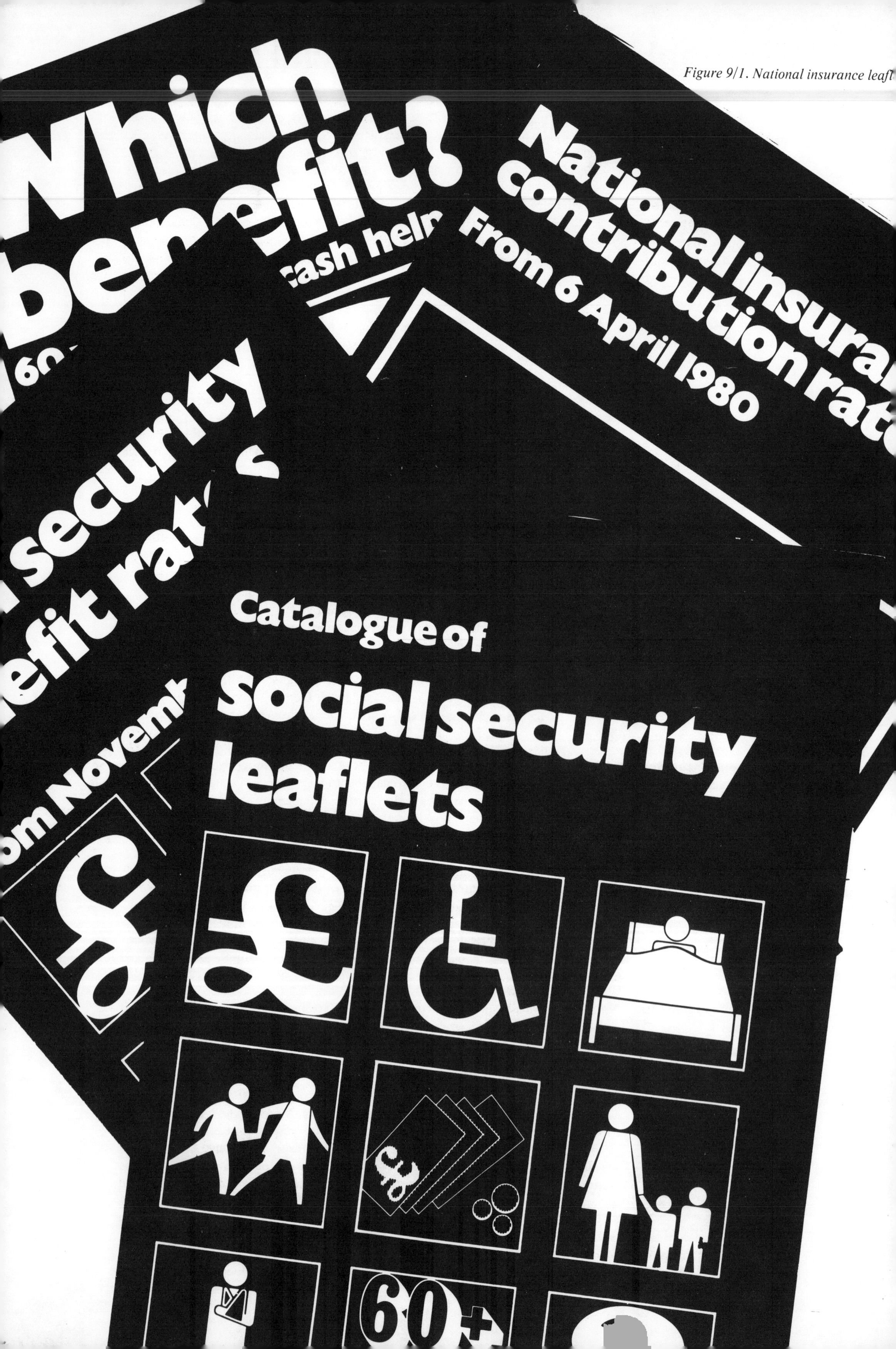

questions will be asked about how much money the person has or expects to have. The mobility allowance for disabled persons is an example of a non-contributory benefit. This allowance is paid to people between the ages of five and sixty-five who are unable or almost unable to walk because of physical disablement. One very common non-contributory benefit at the moment is the Youth Training Scheme (YTS).

9B1C. Means tested benefits

In this category fall a large number of benefits which are only payable after enquiries have been made into a person's background. The means test implies an examination of the current income and expenditure of the person in addition to any funds he may have accumulated. Family Income Supplement (FIS) is a means tested benefit. People on low earnings from their full time employment can claim an allowance dependent on family circumstances and the number of children. Rent and rates rebates, school uniform grants, and student grants are further examples of means tested benefits.

9B2. How the scheme operates

In general everyone in Britain pays National Insurance contributions if they are sixteen or over and employed with earnings above a minimum level or alternatively are self-employed. It is these contributions together with employers' payments and State contributions that pay for benefits. Rates of contributions do change and schedules are available from the Department of Health and Social Security.

As we saw when we looked at the benefits, it is possible to get certain benefits without having made any contributions. Those who do contribute do so in one of four classes:

— *Class 1 contributions* are paid by employees and their employers. The contributions are calculated on gross pay and are collected through PAYE income tax arrangements. The contributions are earnings related.
— *Class 2 contributions* are paid by self-employed people, normally by direct debit to a bank or by stamping a contribution card.
— *Class 3 contributions* are voluntary and can be paid to enable a person to qualify for extra benefits.
— *Class 4 contributions* are paid by self-employed people when profits are over a specified level in any tax year.

A record of the contributions paid by each person is kept. This is done by providing everyone with a national insurance number when they leave school. This number remains with them for the rest of their lives and by referring to it the authorities can check on entitlement to those benefits dependent upon contributions.

9B3. The range of benefits

A whole range of benefits exists in excess of sixty as we mentioned earlier. Figure 9/2 shows a number of the more common benefits with a note as to whether they are benefits which rely on contributions having been paid, are paid regardless of contributions or are means tested.

Figure 9/2. Examples of benefits

Many of these benefits indicate in their name the need they intend to meet. It is difficult, however, to condense a description of the benefits in view of the many conditions, exceptions and qualifications to entitlement which exist. The interested reader is referred to the many useful leaflets produced by DHSS both for detailed descriptions of benefits and current financial amounts payable.

9C. Comparison with commercial insurance

While it is not necessary for us to consider the National Insurance scheme in any more detail it will serve to complete our discussion of it if we identify the ways in which it differs from commercial insurance operations:

(*a*) It is administered by government, the Department of Health and Social Security.

(*b*) The rate of contributions and benefits may be altered by government through Acts of Parliament.

(*c*) The State can, by direct grants, supplement the amount paid in by way of contributions.

(*d*) The State guarantees the solvency of the scheme.

(*e*) It is compulsory that all join the scheme, subject to certain exceptions.

(*f*) The rates of contributions vary according to class but are standard among those within each class. There is no underwriting of risks.

(*g*) No policy is issued and substantial savings accrue due to this.

(*h*) Contributions (premiums) are deducted from earnings, in most cases, at source.

(*i*) Disputes are handled by local tribunals and ultimately a National Insurance Commissioner, not through the courts.

List of statutes

Assurance Companies Act 1909, 7A1B
Assurance Companies Act 1946, 7A1D
Assurance Companies (Winding Up) Acts, 1933–35, 7A1D

Boiler Explosions Act 1882, 3C2B

Companies Act 1967, 7A1F

Elizabethan Poor Law Act 1601, 9A1
Employers' Liability Act 1880, 3E1B
Employers' Liability (Compulsory Insurance) Act 1969, 3E1B, 7E2
Employers' Liability Insurance Companies Act 1907, 7A1A

Finance Act 1976, 4B13E

Industrial Assurance Act 1923, 7A1C
Insurance Brokers (Registration) Act 1977, 5C3, 5G2A, 7D
Insurance Companies Act 1958, 7A1E
Insurance Companies Act 1974, 5G2A, 7A1G, 7B1A
Insurance Companies Act 1981, 7A1G
Insurance Companies Act 1982, 7A1G, 7B
Insurance Companies (Advertisements) (Amendment) Regulations 1983, 7B5
Insurance Companies Amendment Act 1973, 7A1F
Insurance Companies (Classes of Business) Regulations 1977, 7B1A
Insurance Companies Regulations 1981, 7B, 7B2

Life Assurance Act 1774, 3D1C
Life Assurance Companies Act 1870, 7A1A
Lloyd's Act 1871, 5D1
Lloyd's Act 1982, 5D1A

Marine Insurance Act 1906, 3B1B
Merchant Shipping (Oil Pollution) Act 1971, 7E6
Merchant Shipping Act 1974, 7E6
Metropolitan Fire Brigade Act 1865, 3C1C
Motor Vehicles (Passenger Insurance) Act 1972, 3E2A

National Insurance Act 1911, 9A2
National Insurance (Industrial Injuries Act) 1946, 3E1B
Nuclear Installations Act 1965, 7E4

Policyholders' Protection Act 1975, 5G2A, 7B5

Riding Establishments Act 1970, 7E3
Road Traffic Act 1930, 3E2
Road Traffic Act 1960, 3E2A
Road Traffic Act 1972, 7E1

Solicitors' Act 1974, 7E5

Theft Act 1968, 3C2A, 4H2

Workmen's Compensation Act 1897, 3E1B

Index